CH

TV TALK

A dictionary of words and phrases
popularized by television

CHAMBERS

CHAMBERS
An imprint of Chambers Harrap Publishers Ltd
7 Hopetoun Crescent
Edinburgh, EH7 4AY

First published by Chambers Harrap Publishers Ltd 2005

© Chambers Harrap Publishers Ltd 2005

A CIP catalogue record for this book is available from the British Library.

ISBN 0550 10172 1

Designed and typeset by Chambers Harrap Publishers Ltd, Edinburgh
Printed and bound by Clays Ltd, St Ives plc

Contributors

Editor
Ian Brookes

Publishing Manager
Patrick White

Text by
Andrew A Holmes
with additional material by
Ian Brookes
Duncan Marshall
Michael Munro
Mary O'Neill
David Reid
Liam Rodger
Howard Sargeant
Anna Stevenson
Patrick White

Editorial Assistance
Vicky Aldus
Lorna Gilmour

Prepress Manager
Sharon McTeir

Prepress Controllers
Vienna Leigh
Kirsteen Wright

Acknowledgements

The editor and compilers are grateful for the advice, comments and suggestions of the following people: Anne Allan, Sarah Barkley, Katie Brooks, Nadia Cornuau, Esther Fulton, Steven Gallon, Andrew Jamieson, Janice McNeillie, Sharon McTeir (who had the original idea for this book), Kate Nicholson, Elaine O'Donoghue, Georges Pilard, Tom Pinder, Wendy Rimmington, Camilla Rockwood, Clair Simpson, Kate Turnbull.

Extract from *The Complete Yes Minister: The Diaries of the Right Hon. James Hacker* by Jonathan Lynn and Anthony Jay reproduced with the permission of BBC Worldwide Limited. Copyright © Jonathan Lynn and Anthony Jay 1984.

Extract from *The Fall and Rise of Reginald Perrin* reprinted by kind permission of Jonathan Clowes Ltd., London, on behalf of David Nobbs.

Extract from *Newman and Baddiel in Pieces* (BBC), written and performed by Rob Newman and David Baddiel, reproduced with the permission of David Baddiel.

Contents

Introduction

Asked in a recent interview about whether he ever got tired of being tagged as the man who popularized the phrase 'I didn't get where I am today ...' in *The Fall and Rise of Reginald Perrin*, writer David Nobbs professed that he was in fact delighted that people still remembered the programme so fondly. 'If nothing else,' he said, 'It proves that the medium of TV isn't totally ephemeral, and that certain things related to it can and do have a life within the collective memory.'

It is certainly true that television has exerted a powerful influence since it became a fixture in Britain's homes in the 1950s. It may be commonly derided as 'telly' or 'the goggle-box', and cited as the root cause of all that is vacuous, slovenly and generally wrong with our society, but it is hard to deny that it has made some colourful contributions to our language and culture.

The words and phrases that we hear on television on Thursday evening become the stuff of our conversations when we meet in the playground, in the workplace and in the pub on Friday. So it is that TV talk makes the jump from the small screen and becomes part of the mainstream of the English language.

Of course, the huge increase in the number of available channels and the advent of video, DVD and other alternative entertainment formats means that TV is no longer quite the shared national pastime that it used to be. Seldom now does a third of the population of Britain tune in to watch the same show at the same time. But even in the multi-channel era, programmes such as *The Weakest Link* and *Little Britain* have managed to generate huge interest and forge instantly recognizable catchphrases that have been repeated everywhere from the school playground to the Houses of Parliament.

The words and phrases discussed in this book were all either coined or popularized by television, yet there is a huge variety of material here, reflecting the diversity of television itself. The book covers six different decades and three continents (with the emphasis on the experience of British viewers) and spans a range of genres including children's entertainment, comedy, current affairs, sport and drama.

Many of the expressions examined in the book are catchphrases that are associated with a particular performer or programme, but which have been repeated so many times that they have developed a life of their own. The book shows how flexible many such phrases have become and how they can now turn up in places that are a long way removed from the original source: a catchphrase from *The Black Adder*, for example, is used in a newspaper article about the rail industry, while one of Kenny Everett's catchphrases turns up in a wine catalogue. Other phrases have established themselves as a standard shorthand to refer to a particular situation, so that saying 'Don't mention the war' or 'I'll get me coat' conveys a cultural message that goes far beyond the literal meaning of the words.

But television has given us other things besides catchphrases. The artefacts of television programmes have also created new items of vocabulary. Without television our language would never have been enriched by the concept of the 'Tardis' or the 'swingometer', nor would we be able to use the names of television characters – Arthur Daley, Alf Garnett, Victor Meldrew – as vivid embodiments of certain types of personality.

Television has also proved enormously successful as a medium for bringing existing words and phrases to a wider audience. Thus the words 'dipstick' and 'plonker' were both used before *Only Fools and Horses*, but it was that programme that cemented their place in the language. *Tinker, Tailor, Solider, Spy* and *House of Cards* were bestselling books before they were serialized on television, but it took the mass exposure of TV to get people talking about 'moles' and to popularize the saying 'You might say that; I couldn't possibly comment.'

TV Talk covers all of these aspects of language and much more besides. The material is arranged in alphabetical order. Most entries discuss a particular word or phrase, but some programmes that have been especially influential are recognized by special panel entries which discuss the show as a whole. For readers seeking items from any programme not given this treatment, an index has been included at the back of the book.

Finally, there is a second type of experience that we absorb through our TV sets: many of the programmes we watch are punctuated by advertisements. Some people would argue that the ingenuity of advertising copywriters has often surpassed that of the programme makers themselves, and adverts have undoubtedly made a significant contribution to the richness of our language. This legacy is acknowledged by a 'commercial break' in the middle of this book which discusses some expressions popularized by television advertising.

xii

PART ONE

Alf Garnett
Till Death Us Do Part

Few television characters have created such a lasting impression that their names have come to embody a certain type of individual, but one that certainly has managed to achieve this feat is **Alf Garnett**, whose name has come to stand for a loud-mouthed person who proclaims bigoted and racist views.

Alf Garnett was the central character in the situation comedy *Till Death Us Do Part*, which ran from 1965 until 1975, and its sequel *In Sickness and In Health*, which was shown between 1985 and 1992. The character was created by Johnny Speight and played by Warren Mitchell. In the pilot episode, broadcast as part of the *Comedy Playhouse* series, Alf was given the surname Ramsey. However, as Alf Ramsey happened to be the name of the England football manager of the time, the surname was soon changed to Garnett.

Alf was a working-class Londoner who lived with his long-suffering wife Else (Dandy Nichols, although this role was taken by Gretchen Franklin in the pilot), progressive-thinking daughter Rita (Una Stubbs), and left-wing son-in-law Mike (Tony Booth). Much of the programme revolved around set-piece tirades in which Alf rejected liberal values and revelled in his own jingoistic and chauvinistic opinions.

Such has been the influence of the show that not only Alf's name, but also some of his favourite insults, have become firmly established in the language. A prime example of the latter is the expression '**silly old moo**', which was his customary mode of address to Else. This phrase was used as a convenient euphemism for 'silly old cow', which was considered an unacceptable thing for a man to say to his wife on television – although the producers did not have similar scruples about some racist slurs that would now be deemed much more offensive.

Similarly, Alf's abusive remarks to his Liverpudlian son-in-law popularized the expression '**Scouse git**'. The adjective 'Scouse' has been applied to the people of Liverpool since the early part of the 20th century – the name comes from a type of stew known as 'lobscouse' which was popular among sailors in that port city – but the influence of the programme has been such that the insulting 'git' has become an almost automatic addition to it.

all done in the best possible taste

The Kenny Everett Television Show

Hollywood films often feature scenes containing gratuitous nudity, sex and violence. Cynics might suggest that such scenes are only included to attract more viewers, but directors and actors are often heard making disingenuous claims that they are essential to the plot. In the 1980s, Kenny Everett satirized this tendency with his creation Cupid Stunt. Miss Stunt, a pneumatic starlet with a penchant for micro skirts, would talk about her latest film and go into enthusiastic detail about each salacious scene. At the denouement of her description, Cupid would cross her legs exaggeratedly, plump her false breasts, and say, '... and it's **all done in the best possible taste!**'

Cupid Stunt was one of a cavalcade of comic characters who featured in *The Kenny Everett Television Show*, broadcast on BBC1 from 1981 to 1988. (Other memorable creations included Sid Snot, General Bombthebastards, Gizzard Puke, Brother Lee Love, and Marcel Wave.) The programme followed a sketch format and developed from Everett's anarchic radio shows and the series he did for Thames Television in 1978, *The Kenny Everett Video Show*. Although it was this earlier show that won him critical acclaim, it was the BBC series that brought Kenny's brand of over-the-top humour to a wider audience.

Cupid Stunt's catchphrase is still heard to this day, usually being used ironically to describe something that is in fact of rather questionable taste. Andrew Davies, who adapted *Tipping the Velvet*, a drama featuring scenes of lesbian love, for the BBC, was subjected to such irony in a headline in the *Western Mail* in September 2002: 'It's all done in the best possible taste, says Welsh author of TV period romp'.

Even the 2004 Oddbins catalogue invoked Cupid Stunt with this description of a rather fruity French red: 'Consistently marvellous, displaying typical Rhone flavours and all done in the best possible taste!'

a local shop for local people
The League of Gentlemen

In this era of vast out-of-town supermarkets and online grocery shopping, what a comfort it is still to be able to enjoy the old-fashioned community spirit of a corner shop, the sort of place that has come to be known to many television viewers as '**a local shop for local people**'.

This expression was popularized by *The League of Gentlemen*, a surreal and often disturbing black comedy which began as a stage show in 1994, moved to BBC Radio 4 and finally transferred to television in 1998. It is set in the (fortunately) fictional northern English town of Royston Vasey, where more than 50 characters (all brought to life by a mere three actors) indulge in quite bizarre, and often downright illegal, activities.

Royston Vasey's local shop (actually perched on a hill outside the town) is run by 'husband and wife' Edward and Tubbs Tattsyrup (played by Reece Shearsmith and Steve Pemberton respectively). The couple, far from being stalwarts of the local community, hide several dark secrets: they are not only husband and wife but also brother and sister; they keep their bestial son David locked in the attic; and they just happen to be psychotic serial killers.

Both Edward and Tubbs fear beyond all else the invasion of their town by outsiders. They greet all customers with the question 'Are you local?', and those who are not are distrustfully informed, 'This is a local shop for local people; there's nothing for you here.' Many unwitting outsiders end up being tortured, burned and killed by the murderous pair. Convinced that every customer must be a troublemaker and a threat to their insular existence, Edward will spot them quietly browsing the shelves and will immediately bluster, 'What's all this shouting? **We'll have no trouble here!**', the latter part of which also very quickly became a favourite catchphrase and is often used by fans of the show as a comment on a noisy or troublesome situation.

and finally
News at Ten

The words '**and finally**' have been used by a number of television programmes as a means of introducing the final item and to indicate to the audience that it is nearly time to put the kettle on. *That's Life* host Esther Rantzen, after exposing yet another case of shoddy workmanship by a double-glazing company, would use this phrase to segue to a chucklesome closing piece (usually a spelling mistake from a local newspaper or a tradesman with a peculiarly apt surname). It also surfaced regularly on the closing news items on *The Two Ronnies* (see page 8).

For most viewers, however, the phrase is indelibly associated with the newsreader Trevor MacDonald, who anchored Independent Television News's flagship programme *News at Ten* from 1992 until its demise in 1999.

However grim the day's news, however high the body count, it was customary to end the broadcast on an upbeat note, and the change in tone from serious news to something a little more light-hearted (the bungee-jumping grandmother, the scout troop who had baked the world's largest sausage roll) would invariably be effected by the two words 'and finally'.

This quite natural linking phrase was much noted and much imitated, but rather than abandon the cliché, the show's producers embraced the phrase and turned it into an integral feature of the programme. The words 'and finally' would even be displayed on the screen behind the newsreader's head as the last item began.

Although *News at Ten* was taken off the air in March 1999, the 'and finally' feature was so popular that it has continued to be used in later Independent Television News programmes, and it has become a standard formula for introducing a light-hearted subject at the end of a meeting or a long communication.

and I mean that most sincerely

Opportunity Knocks

Hosting a talent show is a tough job. You have to stay enthusiastic at all times and provide equal encouragement to all the performers who come on, no matter how disastrous their act may turn out to be. And if you can manage all that, you then get saddled with some catchphrase that you never even said in the first place.

Such was the fate of Hughie Green, who presented *Opportunity Knocks* on ITV from 1956 to 1978. Each week the show gave six unknown entertainers the chance to appear on television, with viewers writing in over the following week to vote for the winner. The idea of a viewers' poll may have been democratic, but TV demands instant gratification, and so the excellence of each performance was also measured on the spot using an audience reaction monitor – memorably dubbed the **clapometer** – which gave a numerical reading based on the loudness of the applause from the studio audience.

Green presided over the assembled dross – Pam Ayres and Bonnie Langford were among the *best* acts to be featured – with catchphrases including 'For you, opportunity knocks', 'This is your show, folks, and I do mean you' and 'It's make-your-mind-up time', but he never in fact used the catchphrase '**and I mean that most sincerely**, folks'. It was, in fact, the impressionist Mike Yarwood who introduced this phrase in his impersonations of Green, but it so encapsulated Hughie's oleaginous door-to-door-salesman persona that it has become forever associated with him.

Anyone who has to go to the trouble of assuring you that he is sincere about what he is telling you is almost certain to arouse suspicion, and so this catchphrase is often associated with con artists, charlatans and generally untrustworthy figures. A notable example of this occurs in Pink Floyd's song 'Have a Cigar' where it is put into the mouth of a gushing record-company executive: 'Well I've always had a deep respect, and I mean that most sincerely. / The band is just fantastic, that is really what I think. / Oh, by the way, which one's Pink?'

... and it's goodnight from him

The Two Ronnies

The pairing of bespectacled comedians Ronnie Barker and Ronnie Corbett in the sketch show *The Two Ronnies* is in the minds of many TV viewers second only to that of the late, great Eric Morecambe and Ernie Wise.

Messrs Barker and Corbett appeared together in 72 one-hour shows on the BBC between 1971 and 1986. The show had a number of memorable features: each one opened and closed with the two Ronnies as serious-faced announcers presenting spoof news items with their hallmark blend of punning dexterity and good old-fashioned smut. The 'announcer' format was adopted to distinguish their opening routine from that of Morecambe and Wise and also apparently for a more prosaic reason: they were unable to think of anything else to open with. At the conclusion of these bookend slots, they would sign off with Corbett saying, 'So, it's goodnight from me...' and Barker chiming in, '... **and it's goodnight from him**. Goodnight!' Not surprisingly, this became their catchphrase and is often copied in a knowing fashion in leave-taking situations.

As well as double-act material in the shows, there were also solo slots for both men: Barker often appeared as some kind of official spokesman to deliver appeals and announcements on behalf of bizarre charities and obscure government departments; Corbett would deliver long, rambling shaggy-dog stories full of tortuous digressions, his diminutive stature emphasized by the huge chair in which he sat.

The programme was boosted by the contributions of scriptwriters of the calibre of Spike Milligan (who wrote the spoof serial 'The Phantom Raspberry Blower of Old London Town'), David Nobbs, and Monty Python members John Cleese, Graham Chapman, Michael Palin and Terry Jones. Another significant contributor was Gerald Wiley, a mysterious figure nobody on the production team had ever met. After years of receiving material of a consistently high standard from Wiley, a meeting was finally set up between him and the rest of the team in a restaurant. At this meeting it transpired that Gerald Wiley was none other than Ronnie Barker.

And now for something completely different
⇨ See **Monty Python's Flying Circus**

8

And this is me

Will the Real Mike Yarwood Please Stand Up?

In the 1960s and 1970s, families around Britain sat transfixed in front of the television every Saturday night as Mike Yarwood morphed seamlessly from Harold Wilson to Albert Steptoe to Frank Spencer in a series of sketches and stand-up routines. However, the main catchphrase of Britain's most popular impressionist was used to introduce the part of his act when he wasn't doing impressions of anyone. At the end of a typical show the star would give a winning smile to the camera and utter the words '**And this is me.**' This would be the cue for Yarwood, who fancied himself as a bit of a crooner, to shed his chameleon skin and perform *in propria persona* a medley of songs from the golden age of swing.

Mike Yarwood first came to prominence in the early 1960s on variety shows such as *Sunday Night at the London Palladium.* By the end of the decade he had his own show, *Will the Real Mike Yarwood Please Stand Up?* on ITV. However, it is his *Mike Yarwood in Persons* shows on the BBC in the 1970s that are best remembered. After Morecambe and Wise jumped ship to ITV, Yarwood was the Corporation's biggest star and was given the primetime slot on Christmas Day for a number of years. Temptation, however, got the better of him and he eventually followed Eric and Ernie over to 'the other side' for a large fee. Although lucrative, the move was not a success. A new generation of sharper and more satirical impressionists, such as Rory Bremner and the *Spitting Image* team, was more to the public's taste in the eighties. Yarwood fell out of favour and has rarely been seen on TV since.

His catchphrase has not been completely forgotten. After the 1985 Live Aid concert in London, the event's main mover Bob Geldof recalled his trepidation at taking to the stage with his slightly fading band The Boomtown Rats. He confessed to worrying that the huge audience might be less than impressed when he switched back to his day job after having been dubbed a saint for his tireless charity work. It might, he feared, have been like that moment when Mike Yarwood said 'And this is me' – and you always wished it wasn't.

Archie Bunker

All in the Family

In Britain a loud-mouthed bigot is sometimes called an Alf Garnett, but in America he is more likely to be referred to as an **Archie Bunker**. Indeed, this name has even made it into some American dictionaries, along with the related concept of Archie Bunkerism.

Archie Bunker was the central character in *All in the Family*, an American adaptation of *Till Death Us Do Part* (see page 3) that was broadcast from 1971 to 1979. In the show Bunker (played by Carroll O'Connor) was an ill-educated blue-collar worker living with his family in Queens, New York. The series broke new ground on American television, being the first situation comedy to tackle such issues as racism and homosexuality. There was also a follow-up series, *Archie Bunker's Place*, which ran from 1979 to 1983, in which the emphasis shifted from Archie's home life to his business venture running a bar.

Although Archie Bunker had the same crass and reactionary opinions as his British counterpart, he also had a softer side, and the audience was encouraged to feel some sympathy for a character who was struggling to keep his family afloat during a period of social upheaval.

The character continues to have a powerful resonance and is still used by Americans as a convenient shorthand for a certain type of working-class male. In the aftermath of the 2004 presidential election, for example, left-wing actress Janeane Garofalo was quoted as cursing the white males whom she held responsible for the re-election of George Bush with the words 'I want the Archie Bunker contingent in the cracker belt to suffer.'

Arthur Daley

Minder

While much of Britain struggled to come to terms with the early years of Thatcherism, one TV character had no such problem. A natural-born entrepreneur, Arthur Daley did his bit for Britain's growing service economy by selling second-hand cars and whatever he could fit into his carefully guarded lockup. His tireless efforts to better himself were not always appreciated by the Inland Revenue nor by rival businessmen, and his relentless pursuit of readies gave him a somewhat tarnished reputation. So when a small businessman is called an **Arthur Daley** it is not usually meant as a compliment.

Minder, running on ITV between 1979 and 1994, more or less spanned the Thatcher era. Starring George Cole as the cunning and cowardly Arthur Daley and Dennis Waterman as his much-put-upon minder Terry McCann, the programme's depiction of wheeling and dealing among low-rent south London traders quickly entered the British consciousness. Left-leaning politicians picked up on this and scored cheap points by comparing their free-market opponents to Daley. On one occasion, Labour heavyweight Denis Healey remarked of Margaret Thatcher that 'She adds the diplomacy of Alf Garnett to the economics of Arthur Daley.'

Besides providing the language with an enduring synonym for a wheeler-dealer, the show spawned two other catchphrases. Arthur referred to his better half – who, in the tradition established by Captain Mainwaring's spouse Elizabeth in *Dad's Army*, was never actually seen on the show – as **her indoors**. This expression, listed as a synonym of 'wife' in some thesauruses, is often reduced to ''er indoors' to reflect its south London origins. Such was the popularity of the expression that in 1983 Messrs Cole and Waterman released a Christmas single called 'What Are We Going to Get for 'Er Indoors?', a festive musical outing that proved a **nice little earner** for the show's two stars. This latter coinage, meaning a successful money-spinning venture, is *Minder*'s other lasting contribution to the English language. It is still in use to this day, as evidenced by a recent news report that described Gwyneth Paltrow's cameo role in the film *Every Word Is True*, which reportedly earned her £2,000,000 for a single day's work, as 'a nice little earner'.

Ay caramba!
⇨ See **The Simpsons**

Back of the net!

I'm Alan Partridge

The master of the mixed metaphor, Alan Partridge, creation of comedian Steve Coogan, began life as a sports reporter on the BBC Radio 4 programme *On the Hour* in 1991. The character blossomed ('like a phoenix taking flight', as Alan might say himself) when he was given his own spoof radio chat show *Knowing Me, Knowing You* in 1992. TV stardom was soon to beckon, and both shows transferred to the small screen in 1994 (*On the Hour* becoming *The Day Today*).

Coogan then revived the character for two series of *I'm Alan Partridge* in 1997 and 2002. These saw Alan's career on a decidedly downward trajectory, with the former TV personality working as a radio presenter in the backwater of Radio Norwich. It was in episode one of the second series, entitled 'The Talented Mr Alan' and first broadcast on 11 November 2002, that Alan uttered the phrase '**Back of the net!**' Visiting his old school to give a talk, he meets a former classmate, now the languages teacher at the school, who once drew a penis on the back of his jacket, for which Alan was caned by the headmaster. In an increasingly tense exchange, Alan feels that he triumphs when, on finding that Phil has an older wife, he says 'My girlfriend's 33. I'm 47. She's 14 years younger than me. Back of the net!' This final exclamation is accompanied by an exuberant swing of his right leg as he scores an imaginary goal.

Although only used that one time, the phrase caught the imagination and is still copied, with the characteristic Partridge intonation, when a telling point has been made, or to celebrate a notable success (rather like 'one-nil', another football phrase). Perhaps it has caught on because it sums up so well the hapless broadcaster's distinctive vainglorious idiom, described by Mark Lawson in *The Guardian* as suggesting 'a half-deaf impressionist giving his Jeremy Clarkson'.

Bada bing!

⇨ See **The Sopranos**

Beam me up, Scotty

Star Trek

One of the distinctive features of the science-fiction show *Star Trek* (see page 174) was that the crew was drawn from all nations: all-American Captain Kirk was supported by people with names such as Chekhov and Sulu, while the ship's chief engineer was an archetypal Scot.

So it comes as something of a disappointment to discover that the actor who played Chief Engineer Montgomery Scott – known as 'Scotty' to his colleagues – was in fact Canadian and not Scottish at all. James Doohan was born in Vancouver in 1920. But he did manage a broad and believable Scots accent for the role, which was heard to best effect when expressing his concern for the state of his engines ('I cannae hold her, cap'n, she's breaking up') and in particular his beloved dilithium crystals. He also displayed his Scottish credentials by playing the bagpipes at Spock's funeral in the second *Star Trek* film, *The Wrath of Khan*.

As the ship's engineer, one of Scotty's jobs was to operate the transporter system that allowed the crew to travel down to the surface of a planet. (Trivia fans should note that those aren't actually James Doohan's hands you see moving the sliders on the transporter console. A hand model had to be used as Doohan had lost the middle finger of his right hand when he took part in the D-Day landings as a soldier in the Royal Canadian Artillery.) Instructions to transport, or 'beam', people up from the planet surface would be delivered in different ways, such as 'Three to beam up' or, in especially dire straits, 'Get us out of here, Mr Scott.' Peculiarly, the phrase that most people associate with this activity, '**Beam me up, Scotty**', was in fact never used in any of the 79 episodes of the original series.

However, perhaps as a result of the many parodies of *Star Trek* that have been written, it is this wording that has stuck in the collective consciousness. It is used as an exclamation of exasperation when you want to be removed instantaneously from an embarrassing, awkward or unpleasant situation. Often this will be because someone has just uttered something very stupid or boring, and it is as if you are talking with someone who is clearly from a different planet.

Bernie the bolt

The Golden Shot

People who are not familiar with *The Golden Shot* might imagine that **Bernie the bolt** is the name of a champion greyhound or perhaps some kind of comedy robot. In fact, the term began as a catchphrase and evolved into a nickname for one of the regulars on this game show.

The Golden Shot, which was aired on ITV from 1967 to 1972, with a brief revival in 1974 and 1975, was based on the firing of a crossbow bolt at a target in order to win prizes. The gimmick was that the crossbow was fixed to a camera in the studio, operated by a blindfolded cameraman who moved it in response to instructions ('Right a bit, left a bit, fire!') phoned in live by contestants at home. Hosts of the show included Jackie Ray, Norman Vaughan, Charlie Williams and Bob Monkhouse, and there were a number of glamorous female assistants – naturally known as 'Golden Girls' – the most famous of whom was Anne Aston. One of the host's tasks was to instruct a studio technician to insert the crossbow bolt into the weapon with the words, 'Bernie, the bolt.' In time it became fixed in the public mind that the person who fired the shot was actually named 'Bernie the bolt', although in fact at least three different people were involved in the process.

Because it had to be done live, the show was always open to mishaps, including one in which a contestant was unable to participate because she had somehow knocked herself unconscious on a visit to the toilet. Another contestant – remember that this was long before the days of mobile phones – took part from a public phonebox while watching a screen in a nearby TV shop.

big girl's blouse
Nearest and Dearest

If a male friend tells you he's afraid of spiders, complains that his new shoes are dirty, or refuses to put the rubbish out on a rainy day because he doesn't want to get his hair wet, you might call him a **big girl's blouse**.

This teasing assault on unmanliness has been around since the late 1960s, with the first recorded example appearing in a 1969 episode of the ITV sitcom *Nearest and Dearest*, which ran from 1969 to 1972. In the series, the ineffectual and workshy Eli Pledge, played by Jimmy Jewel, is regularly rounded on by his no-nonsense spinster sister Nellie, played by the scene-stealing Hylda Baker at her pocket-battleship best. Set in a small Lancashire town, where the pair have inherited a pickle-bottling factory, the programme's stock-in-trade was rapid-fire banter laced with innuendo, the bawdiness fuelled by Nellie's sexual frustration and much of the comedy deriving from her frequent malapropisms.

As an insult, 'big girl's blouse' clearly belongs to the group of expressions that ridicule men by referring to them as women or girls. It's not clear why the word 'blouse' should have been added to the older taunt of 'big girl', but its feminine nature is presumably intended to reinforce the ridicule. Neither is it entirely clear whether, in using the expression, you are dismissing a man as the big blouse of a girl, or the blouse of a big girl, but, if it's the former, perhaps the expression also communicates something of the notion of panicking or 'flapping'.

Big hug!

Teletubbies

The expression '**Big hug!**' is probably the most noteworthy contribution to the English language made by the children's television programme *Teletubbies*, which was first broadcast in 1997. The show was created by Anne Wood, and caused something of a stir when it was first broadcast for its supposedly low educational content.

The series featured four brightly coloured creatures, Dipsy (green), Laa-Laa (yellow), Tinky-Winky (purple), and Po (red), who lived inside a hill and communicated in a series of childish utterances. Amongst the more coherent of these was 'Big hug!' which acted as a signal for the Teletubbies to embrace each other, something they did frequently and enthusiastically.

As Britons have become more tactile, and a full embrace has become a viable alternative to a firm handshake in some social situations, so the phrase 'Big hug!' has been taken up as a light-hearted and unthreatening means of inviting or accepting this sort of greeting.

Another element of the Teletubbies' language which caught on was the use of '**Eh-oh**' as a substitute for 'hello'. This latter phrase was further popularized by the hit record 'Teletubbies Say "Eh-oh"' which set the musings of the Teletubbies to a rave beat and so cashed in on the programme's cult following among students in the late 1990s.

bionic
The Six Million Dollar Man

In science, bionics is 'the study of how living organisms function, and the application of the principles observed to develop computers and other machines which work in similar ways'. In science fiction, the word '**bionic**' is used to refer to people with mechanical body parts that give them superhuman powers of strength, speed and endurance. This latter meaning was popularized by an American TV programme which required the audience to suspend its disbelief when a man was able to prevent a helicopter from taking off merely by hanging onto it with one arm.

The Six Million Dollar Man concerned the phenomenal exploits of Steve Austin (played by Lee Majors), a man whose shattered body is rebuilt with biomechanical technology following the crash of his experimental aircraft. Not only does the surgery save his life, but it also gives him incredible powers which are put to good use by his new employers, the Office of Scientific Intelligence. After three pilot episodes in 1973, the show ran for five seasons between 1974 and 1978, and even spawned a sequel, *The Bionic Woman*. This spin-off featured Austin's love interest, Jaime Sommers (played by Lindsay Wagner), and featured the same sort of exploits but performed by a woman.

The show was initially successful, but by 1978 it had strained credibility too far and was cancelled. Viewers could probably sense the end was coming when they were first treated to a plotline that had the mythical creature Bigfoot in league with space aliens, and then confronted by the appearance on the show of a bionic dog called Max-a-million. Lee Majors' ill-advised decision to grow a moustache was just about the final nail in the show's coffin.

⇨ See also **We have the technology**

Blue Peter

The 21st of November is a notorious date in the annals of TV history. For it was on this day in 1983 that Janet Ellis, in grave tones reminiscent of those used by Neville Chamberlain to announce Britain's declaration of war on Germany, told a shocked public that the *Blue Peter* garden had been vandalized. The nation's outrage at this wanton criminal damage did not abate over the years. In 2000, when Premiership footballer Les Ferdinand admitted he had been part of the gang that had perpetrated the attack, a furious editorial in *The Sun* demanded that he give *Blue Peter* compensation for the atrocity.

Few if any children's programmes have made an impact like that of *Blue Peter*. First broadcast in 1958, and edited for many years by the formidable Biddy Baxter, it has steadfastly stuck to a Reithian remit of enlightening, educating and entertaining its young audience, presenting them with a range of informative features in a magazine format. Its most memorable moments, however, are perhaps those which might have had the BBC's stern Caledonian founder spinning in his grave. The incontinent behaviour of Lulu, a Sri Lankan baby elephant who left an unexpected gift on the studio floor, is often cited as one of TV's funniest moments, while the broken bones of John Noakes and Janet Ellis are testimony to the numerous daredevil stunts performed by the presenters over the years.

It is not just skydiving and tobogganing techniques that a *Blue Peter* presenter must master. Constructing models of the International Space Station or the Sydney Opera House using only empty washing-up-liquid bottles and the ubiquitous **sticky-back plastic** – a term coined in an attempt to avoid endorsing any commercial product, which went on to become synonymous with *Blue Peter* – is also a key skill. The creation of such models live in front of the cameras can lead to occasional mishaps, but if these should happen presenters can quickly put aside their own ham-fisted efforts and replace them with much better versions, using the famous words **'Here's one I made earlier.'**

The formula has become so recognizable that *The Sun* could pick up on it in 2004 as part of an affectionate parody in which former presenter Janet Ellis was enlisted to make a model of *Blue Peter*'s newest recruit: '*Blue Peter* is turning into *Phew Peter* after signing up ex-beauty-queen Zoe Salmon as a presenter. And to celebrate here's one your *Sun* has made earlier than anyone else – a fantastic model of sexy Zoe put together with sticky-back plastic.'

Although the programme will always be associated with crude model-making and mishaps with animals, it must be remembered that *Blue Peter* has done a great deal of public-spirited work over the years. Its annual appeals have not only raised money for such deserving causes as Romanian orphans and the victims of Pol Pot's regime in Cambodia, they have also made children aware of their responsibilities to those less fortunate. The show has regularly rewarded acts of courage and philanthropy by viewers with the presentation of a **Blue Peter badge**. The badge features the programme's sailing ship logo, designed by Tony Hart, and it must be worn by all presenters whenever they are in front of a camera. Regular viewers will know that there is a hierarchy of *Blue Peter* badges: the plain blue one is a reward for sending in a letter or a poem; the green one recognizes acts of environmental awareness; while the gold *Blue Peter* badge is the show's equivalent of the Victoria Cross and is only rarely awarded.

Bolly

Absolutely Fabulous

Media people in London are notoriously thirsty. However, their obsession with being seen near the right labels means that only certain upmarket beverages will satisfy them. Edina Monsoon and Patsy Stone were no different, and their penchant for **Bolly** (Bollinger champagne), **Stolly** (Stolichnaya vodka) and other expensive drinks was clear to anyone having to wade through the empties in Edina's living room the morning after a typical binge.

Absolutely Fabulous, a British sitcom first aired by the BBC in 1992, satirized the vacuous and desperately trendy lives of the 'sweeties' and 'darlings' who constitute the London media and PR world. Edina (Jennifer Saunders) and Patsy (Joanna Lumley), despite their advancing years, still like to party like it's 1969. However, their hedonistic activities always catch up with them, resulting in stern lectures, in a clever piece of generational role reversal, from Edina's sensible but prudish daughter Saffron (Julia Sawalha). Veteran actress June Whitfield (playing Edina's mother) often stole the show with her deflating comments.

Absolutely Fabulous was immensely popular, its name being shortened affectionately to *AbFab* by its legion of fans. At the height of their popularity, the cast of the show even recorded a single with synthesizer group The Pet Shop Boys entitled, not surprisingly, 'Absolutely Fabulous'.

Book him, Danno

Hawaii Five-0

The words '**Book him, Danno**' were frequently uttered by Jack Lord in his role as Detective Steve McGarrett in *Hawaii Five-O*, which ran for 12 seasons between 1968 and 1980, making it the longest-running police drama in American television history. Tight-lipped McGarrett was the head of an elite police unit investigating 'organized crime, murder, assassination attempts, foreign agents, felonies of every type'. He was ably assisted by the target of his terse catchphrase, Detective Danny Williams (played until the show's penultimate season by James MacArthur). The words fell from McGarrett's lips every time they got the bad guy, which turned out to be pretty much every episode.

Lord's role in the series went beyond playing the lead character: his contract also gave him considerable editorial control, and it was he who insisted, against the wishes of the CBS network, that it be shot entirely on location in Hawaii. He also employed numerous local residents in acting roles. As it turned out, this move not only enhanced the show's appeal by accentuating its exotic setting and characters, but also boosted the Hawaiian economy. CBS's spending on production and on the living expenses of the cast and crew was estimated at more than $100 million a year, and the show was also credited with generating a significant increase in tourism to the islands. Lord and his wife Marie actually moved to Hawaii from New York during the show's early years, and never left; Lord died there in January 1998 at the age of 77.

Long after the show's demise, 'Book him, Danno' remains a popular headline for articles about football matches which involve numerous bookings. It was used in this context, for example, in a piece about the Germany–Cameroon match in the 2002 World Cup. In this game the Spanish referee Antonio Jesus Lopez Nieto handed out 16 yellow cards, which roughly comes to one every six minutes and is a World Cup record. (In case you were wondering, Germany won 2–0.)

Boom, boom!

The Basil Brush Show

Few glove puppets can boast of performances at both Buckingham Palace and Downing Street. Basil Brush belongs to that select pantheon of performers, delighting Prince William on his fifth birthday and cheering up Prime Minister Jim Callaghan, no doubt with jokes underlined by his trademark cry of '**Boom, boom!**'

The irrepressible fox was brought to life in 1963 by Peter Firmin (co-creator of *Bagpuss* and *The Clangers*) on commercial television in *The Three Scampis* and later appeared on *The Nixon Line*, in which he provided comic counterpoint to the tricks of magician David Nixon. He was then lured to the BBC where his eponymous show ran from 1968 to 1980. Basil was accompanied by a series of straight-men – Mr Rodney (Rodney Bewes), Mr Derek (Derek Fowlds), Mr Roy (Roy North), Mr Howard (Howard Williams) and Mr Billy (Billy Boyle) – whom he interrupted constantly with his corny music-hall gags. Dressed like an Edwardian gentleman, Basil possessed an aristocratic accent similar to that of Terry-Thomas. Ivan Owen provided this distinctive voice but kept very much behind the scenes, refusing to appear with his alter ego in case he broke the illusion that Basil was a real fox.

Owen died in 2000 and that appeared to have put an end to Basil's career. But in 2002 the vulpine puppet resurfaced on the BBC in a children's sitcom, also called *The Basil Brush Show*. However, the creators of the new show, Entertainment Rights plc, refused to reveal the identity of the new man behind the voice, explaining that the voice was provided by 'Basil Brush himself'.

Booyakasha!
The 11 O'Clock Show

Channel 4's 'voice of youth', Ali G's mission is to bring the language of the streets to a wider audience. Thanks to his work, '**Booyakasha!**' (a greeting intended to imitate the blast and recoil of a powerful gun) has now become part of the English language.

Ali G started life as part of the topical late-night comedy of *The 11 O'Clock Show*, first broadcast in 1998. The show itself is not considered a classic, but it did launch the careers of two comics who would be enormously influential over the next decade: Ricky Gervais (star of *The Office*) and Sacha Baron Cohen, the creator of Ali G.

The character of Ali G is intended to satirize 'wiggers', young white men who have adopted the clothes, speech patterns and recreational interests of black gangsta rappers. Ali is a white youth who lives in the rather dull London suburb of Staines. In his own mind, though, he and his friends in the West Staines **massive** (supposedly an intimidating street gang) are living in an exciting black ghetto dominated by drugs and guns. If Ali feels that someone is not giving him enough respect he assumes that there might be a 'racialist' motive, asking the question '**Is it because I is black?**'

Although the character is played by a Jewish comedian, Ali G is an Asian-sounding fictional name that has been adopted by a white man who thinks he is black. Most people understand the joke, but there are two particular groups who don't 'get' Ali G. The first consists of those who think that Ali G is satirizing black culture itself rather than the suburban white youths who adopt it. The second comprises Ali G's victims: the politicians, scientists, judges and the like who are so detached from youth culture that they think Ali G is a real TV presenter and who are usually too polite to criticize him when he confronts them with deliberately ignorant and offensive remarks.

Ali G has quickly become a comic icon, so much so that other TV comedies can refer to him without confusing their own audiences. Antony, the son in *The Royle Family*, irritates his older relatives when he and his friend quote lengthy passages from an Ali G programme. In Slough, meanwhile, Keith turns up at *The Office* on Red Nose Day dressed as Ali G, raising money for charity by answering his phone throughout the day with a greeting of 'Booyakasha!'

Brookside

A soap opera can perhaps consider itself to have 'arrived' only once it is the subject of pastiches by other television programmes. In the 1990s, *Brookside* was memorably sent up on *Harry Enfield's Television Programme* in a lampoon called *Breadside* which featured a quarrelsome trio known as the Scousers (see page 62). Their speech was liberally sprinkled with Scouse slang, but when the Scousers used such words as 'kecks', 'la' and 'bizzy', non-Liverpudlians were not left scratching their heads – they had become accustomed to such language through exposure to *Brookside*.

When Channel 4 was launched in 1982, *Brookside* was one the first programmes it showed. A soap opera set in the Croxteth suburb of Liverpool, it quickly became one of the channel's most popular shows – and also one of the most controversial. Phil Redmond, the show's creator, was determined to break taboos and tackle subjects from which other soaps shied away. In 1994 a gay female relationship was depicted; and two years later the show had a plotline revolving around incest. Whether this was for public-spirited reasons or merely the desire to boost ratings is open to question.

In 2003, after twenty-one years of murders, affairs, lesbian kisses, and hostage-takings, *Brookie* was finally pensioned off by Channel 4. For launching the singing careers of Jennifer Ellison and Claire Sweeney, that might be considered a firm but fair punishment.

A *Brookside* glossary

bizzy	*a policeman*
Chrizzy	*Christmas*
come 'ed	*an invitation to start fighting*
divvy	*a stupid person*
do one	*to run away (a short form of 'do a runner')*
'ead the ball	*a stupid or brain-damaged person*
have a cob on	*to be in a bad mood*
it's doin' me 'ead in	*it is disturbing my emotional stability*
kecks	*trousers*
kidder	*an affectionate term of address*
la	*a friend*
leccy	*electricity*
made up	*very happy*
me old feller	*my father*
moby	*a mobile shop*
on the bevvy	*out drinking*
oppo	*a surgical operation*
our kid	*my younger brother*
ozzie	*a hospital*
scally	*an antisocial young person*
soash	*social security*
soft lad	*an insulting term of address*
sound	*very good*

Buffy the Vampire Slayer

From humble beginnings *Buffy the Vampire Slayer* became one of the most successful TV shows of recent history. Running for seven seasons between 1997 and 2003, initially on the Warner Brothers network and later on UPN, the series gained a huge cult following and much critical acclaim, notably for its witty scripts and sassy star Sarah Michelle Gellar.

Created by Joss Whedon, whose writing credits included the films *Speed* (1994) and *Toy Story* (1995) and the TV series *Roseanne* (1988–97), Buffy Summers experienced an inauspicious start to her career. Whedon wrote the screenplay for the original *Buffy the Vampire Slayer* film, which flopped on its release in 1992. It wasn't until 1997 that he fully realized his vision for the character; assembling a team of writers, including himself, he became executive producer of the TV show that was to resurrect the teenage heroine.

The series is set in the Californian suburb of Sunnydale, located above a 'Hellmouth' which regularly unleashes hordes of vampires, demons and general badness into the world. Buffy is the Chosen One, who alone has been granted special powers and a calling to spend her short life fighting the forces of evil which threaten her home and the world. Between times she manages to balance her studies, teenage social activities and a complicated love life.

The striking contrast of themes is also reflected in the language used in the show. Buffy and her friends mix the traditional lexicon of the horror genre with playful Californian teen-speak and popular culture references, creating a vocabulary that is unique, current and very smart. Much of the language draws heavily on Whedon's own idiosyncratic verbal style and has developed with the characters over the course of the show's run, earning the writer an Emmy nomination in 2000 for Outstanding Writing for a Drama Series.

A *Buffy* glossary

badness	*evil*
bite-fest	*a vampire's killing frenzy*
break-and-enterish	*(of clothing) making the wearer look like a criminal*
carbon-dated	*very old*
clueage	*evidence*
cuddle-monkey	*a boyfriend*
dateville	*the fictional world of a romantically involved couple*
dusting	*the act of killing vampires or demons*
freaky-deaky	*crazy, odd*
guiltapalooza	*extreme guilt*
a happy	*an ephemeral pleasant episode*
Heart-of-Darknessy	*dark and depressing*
lunchable	*1. tasty; 2. sexually appealing*
my bad	*my mistake*
pointy	*the opposite of pointless*
Sabrina	*a witch (alluding to the comedy series Sabrina the Teenage Witch)*
single entendre	*a statement of the blatantly obvious*
sitch	*a situation*
slayage	*the killing of vampires and demons*
slut-o-rama	*a woman of dubious morals*
übersuck	*a situation that is as bad as it gets*
unbendy	*straight*
Undead American	*a politically correct term for an American vampire*
vague up	*to make something more confusing*
the wacky	*odd behaviour*
wiggins	*a moment of fear or panic*
wow-potential	*sexual attractiveness*

But we don't want to give you that
⇨ See **Who Wants to Be a Millionaire?**

Calm down! Calm down!
⇨ See **Harry Enfield's Television Programme**

Can we fix it? Yes we can!
Bob the Builder

Animated daytime television shows are supposed to be comforting fantasies for young children. Yet *Bob the Builder* seems to be aimed at adults. The show's protagonist is a friendly and efficient tradesman who arrives promptly in response to a call, does the job quickly, and does not charge an arm and a leg for his services. His refreshing 'can-do' attitude is summed up in a catchphrase which few builders in the real world would ever utter: '**Can we fix it? Yes we can!**'

Bob the Builder is a stop-motion animated series first shown by the BBC in 1997. Each episode features Bob (voiced by Neil Morrissey) and his team of anthropomorphized vehicles building, fixing and repairing all manner of things to a high standard. The work is never botched and Bob has never been taken by a customer to the Small Claims Court. Such quality workmanship has made Bob hugely popular and he has cashed in on his success with two chart-topping hits. 'Can We Fix It? Yes We Can' was a Christmas number one in 2000, and Bob's cover of Lou Bega's 'Mambo No. 5' was an equally successful follow-up in 2001.

Bob's catchphrase has spread beyond the programme and is now often heard when people are urging a positive approach to an apparently intractable problem. In August 2004, for example, *The Guardian* used it as the headline for a story setting out proposals for improvements in the standard of nursery care. But the following month the *Ealing Times* had a rather more negative take on the phrase when it bemoaned the country's ineptitude at DIY in an article entitled 'Can we fix it? No we can't!'

Can you tell what it is yet?

Hey Presto – It's Rolf

Budding art connoisseurs in the 1960s and 1970s could count themselves lucky. At tea-time on Saturday they would be treated to a masterclass by Antipodean entertainer Rolf Harris, who would paint his murals in such a way as to disguise the subject matter until the piece was almost finished. During the painting of the artwork, Harris would turn round to the enrapt but bemused audience and ask the question '**Can you tell what is yet?**', knowing full well that they couldn't.

Born in Australia, Rolf Harris moved to Britain in 1952 and has enjoyed over five decades as one of television's most versatile performers. As a musician he has had chart success on a number of occasions, including a seven-week run at number one in 1969 with 'Two Little Boys' and an unlikely top-ten hit with a cover of Led Zeppelin's 'Stairway to Heaven'. This most recent hit featured Harris playing the wobble board, an instrument he invented and which appeared on perhaps his most famous single, 'Tie Me Kangaroo Down, Sport'. As an artist he is best known for the murals he painted on his children's variety shows *Hey Presto – It's Rolf* (1966), *The Rolf Harris Show* (1966–71) and *Rolf on Saturday – OK?* (1977–79). Usually of an outback landscape and often inspired by Aboriginal art, their creation formed the centrepiece of Rolf's programmes and provided the source of his catchphrase which, in 2002, was used as the title of his autobiography.

Moreover, the phrase is also routinely used – often pronounced with an Australian accent in homage to its creator – when people are demonstrating anything whose intended final form remains unclear, such as a dish in the early stages of being cooked or a tune tentatively picked out on the piano.

cheap as chips
Bargain Hunt

Winner of 'Most Popular Daytime Programme' in the prestigious National Television Awards of 2002, *Bargain Hunt* has been referred to as the jewel in the crown of daytime TV. The first series aired in Spring 2000 and introduced the viewing public to flamboyant antiques dealer David Dickinson and his catchphrase **'cheap as chips'.** Dickinson himself received the accolade 'Greatest Living Englishman Number 72' from *Loaded* magazine. The citation for this award referred to Mr Dickinson as 'tobacco permatanned, with a proud badger bouffant ...like a mutant hybrid of Arthur Daley and some check-clothed thing out of *The Wind in the Willows*'. As if this were not enough, he made the front cover of the *Radio Times* in December 2002, and caused a media sensation when he posed nude for the magazine.

In the 'laugh and learn' *Bargain Hunt* programme, two teams of amateur antiques collectors are given £500 and just one hour to visit an antiques fair and find themselves a bargain. About a week later the items they bought are offered for auction, and the team that makes the greatest profit (or loses the least amount of money) is declared the winner, with any profit being shared out among the team members.

Dickinson's alliteratively chirpy catchphrase is now widely used to refer to anything that's a bit of a bargain, though you might be surprised to learn that he is not the phrase's originator. Cheap as Chips is the name of a discount retail chain in South Australia, with 22 stores and around 600 staff. Selling anything from greeting cards to furnishings to car accessories, its buyers scour the world for bargains. Now celebrating over 20 years in business, the owner started selling from the boot of his car, and has almost certainly not posed nude in order to further his career.

Check, please!

Goodness Gracious Me

Despite originally being written for television, the sketch show *Goodness Gracious Me* first aired as a radio pilot – a cheap way of demonstrating its potential to a BBC producer cautious about the appeal of a show that uses the experience of British Asians as the starting point for many of its jokes. The pilot led to a full radio series, which duly went on to win a Sony Award, before the show was moved to TV.

Since the move to TV in 1998, there have been three six-programme series and two specials, featuring the talents of Sanjeev Bhaskar, Kulvinder Ghir, Meera Syal and Nadia Wadia, as well as Roger Lamb (often referred to in the show's publicity as 'the token white bloke'). The show's title alludes to the hit comedy record 'Goodness Gracious Me' made by Peter Sellers and Sophia Loren to promote the 1960 film *The Millionairess*, in which Sellers, in brownface make-up, played an Indian doctor.

Rather like *The Fast Show* (see page 183), *Goodness Gracious Me* uses a sketch format that trades on the viewers' familiarity with recurring characters and their catchphrases. These include Smeeta Smitten, Showbiz Kitten, a Bollywood gossip columnist; the Westwardly-mobile Kapoor family, so desperate to shed all traces of their Indian heritage that they pronounce their name 'Cooper'; and the toe-curlingly tactless suitor who manages to offend every girl he dines with, leaving him alone in the restaurant forlornly raising his arm and calling, '**Check, please!**' This last phrase proved so successful that it now vies with 'I'll get me coat' (see page 76) as the phrase most likely to come to mind whenever you have just subjected yourself to complete and utter humiliation.

Chewbacca defence

⇨ See **South Park**

31

Chrismukkah
⇨ See **The OC**

clapometer
⇨ See **and I mean that most sincerely**

Clunk click every trip
Public Information Film

It seems hard to believe now, but it was not until 1965 that every car built in Europe had to come fitted with front seat belts. Increasing car use in the 1950s and 1960s produced a dramatic rise in road accidents, with many deaths resulting from drivers being thrown through the front windscreen. To tackle this problem the Royal Society for the Prevention of Accidents sponsored a series of public safety information films to increase awareness of the importance of using seat belts. The films were first broadcast on television in 1971, and featured DJ and presenter Jimmy Savile, who used the slogan '**Clunk click every trip**' to ram home the message. Drivers were exhorted to 'clunk the door' and 'click the seat belt' before starting their journey. The films were a success, and driving without a seat belt became less common over the next decade.

By January 1983 it was an offence not to belt up in the front seat of a car, and in 1991 the use of rear seat belts became compulsory too. But even in this era of compulsory seat belts, Jimmy Savile's catchphrase is often echoed by drivers when checking with passengers if they have 'clunk-clicked' before the start of a journey.

Come on down!

The Price Is Right

Before the mid-1980s, the contestants on British quiz shows might have been forgiven for casting jealous eyes at their counterparts in America, where game shows were famed for big prizes and for the wild enthusiasm of their audiences. British quiz shows, on the other hand, were more sedate and the rewards rather modest: contestants on shows such as *Sale of the Century* could expect little more than gentle ripples of applause to greet the winning of a Teasmade or novelty toast rack. But all that changed in 1984 as America's most talked about game show *The Price Is Right* crossed the Atlantic and got British people to throw off their inhibitions as soon as they heard the words '**Come on down!**'

This was the greeting Leslie Crowther (and later Bruce Forsyth) used to summon a quartet of people from the audience to Contestants' Row at the start of the show. Selection was random and, by the time their names were announced by the host, the fortunate four were in a state of delirious excitement, as was the rest of the audience. The contestants then played games with names such as 'Hole in One', 'Plinko', 'Cliffhanger' and 'Switcheroo', all designed to test their knowledge of the sale price of various goods. Consumer durables, cash and a big prize at the end were on offer in what was then Britain's richest game show.

So just how did the show's makers turn a reticent British audience into a frenzied mob? Producer William G Stewart, who later became host of the more cerebral quiz *Fifteen to One*, has since revealed that his secret weapon was Edward Elgar. Noting the effect that 'Land of Hope and Glory' had on the crowd at the Last Night of the Proms, Stewart played the stirring march at full volume before filming started. The music did its job, and by the time the quiz began the audience members could barely contain themselves.

correctamundo

Happy Days

The character of Fonzie in the long-running American sitcom *Happy Days* was so cool that he could often express a wealth of emotion with the single syllable 'Hey!' (see page 67). On occasions when more complex vocabulary was required, he demonstrated a penchant for emphasizing words by means of the cod-Italian suffix '-mundo'. Thus 'fabamundo' meant 'very good', 'coolamundo' meant 'very cool' and '**correctamundo**' meant 'absolutely correct'.

The last of these coinages received an unexpected new lease of life in 1994 when it was used in Quentin Tarantino's film *Pulp Fiction*. In the film, the ultra-hip character of Jules Winnfield (played by Samuel L Jackson) attempts to instil calm when confronted by a hysterical armed robber (Amanda Plummer). He encourages her to be cool 'like Fonzie', and when he asks, 'What's Fonzie like?' and receives the answer 'cool', he reassures her by saying, 'Correctamundo!'

The fact that the word 'correctamundo' was used by not one but two of the coolest characters in 20th-century popular drama has encouraged a number of people to use it themselves in the hope that some of the coolness would rub off on them. If only it were that easy.

corridor of uncertainty
⇨ See **Snickometer®**

Cosmopolitan

Sex and the City

Television has long been known as the perfect medium for making your product known to millions. An endorsement from a TV lifestyle guru such as Delia Smith or her American counterpart Martha Stewart can trigger a feeding frenzy that sees shelves stripped bare in a matter of seconds. Even fictional TV programmes can sometimes influence what we buy in the high street: *Miami Vice* popularized the white slip-on shoe, while *Dynasty* began the fashion for big hair and shoulder pads.

When it comes to starting trends, though, the American drama series *Sex and the City* is in a league of its own. At the height of the show's popularity, retailers spoke of the 'Carrie effect', in which anything worn by the lead character one day flew off the shelves the next. Demand for Carrie's favourite footwear, particularly Jimmy Choos and Manolo Blahniks – which gained such recognition that they became known simply as **Manolos** – also increased dramatically during the show's run. It wasn't just clothes and shoes, however. The **Cosmopolitan**, the favourite cocktail of Carrie and her friends, is now well known to barmen throughout the world, and is an essential start to any self-respecting girls' night out.

Sex and the City, which ran from 1998 to 2004, depicted the complicated love lives of four glamorous thirtysomething Manhattanites, Carrie (Sarah Jessica Parker), Miranda (Cynthia Nixon), Samantha (Kim Catrall) and Charlotte (Kristin Davies). The series was adapted from the newspaper columns and book of Candace Bushnell, upon whom the character of Carrie is based. *Sex and the City* combined clever dialogue with frank discussions of sex and musings on the importance of friends and the difficulties of finding the perfect man. The final episode was greeted with sadness by its fans, many of whom gathered at themed parties to toast their departing heroines with a Cosmopolitan or two.

> To make a Cosmopolitan you will require:
>
> 1 oz Vodka
> ½ oz Triple sec
> ½ oz Rose's® Lime Juice
> ½ oz Cranberry juice
> Lime wedge

Cowabunga!

Teenage Mutant Ninja Turtles

Would you adopt a slogan uttered by a bizarre character that was a cross between a turtle and a human teenager? Millions of kids did in the 1980s and 1990s, crying out '**Cowabunga!**' along with their heroes, the *Teenage Mutant Ninja Turtles*.

This was a highly popular comic book that became an animated series on TV (first screened in America in 1987). The story concerned four ordinary turtles who, in that great standby of the world of superheroes, were accidentally exposed to radiation, turning them into half-human creatures. They were taken under the wing of Master Splinter, a similarly mutated rat who by a happy coincidence was a *sensei* able to instruct them in ninja martial arts. These skills came in handy in their battles against their arch-enemies, the evil brain-like Krang and the merciless Shredder. Strangely enough, when the programme was first aired in the UK it was retitled *Teenage Mutant Hero Turtles* because of a current scare about the use of ninja-style weapons amongst youth gangs.

When not fighting crime, the Turtles, named Michelangelo, Leonardo, Raphael and Donatello, liked to eat pizza and go surfing and it is from the latter activity that the triumphant exclamation 'Cowabunga!' springs. American surfers were using this in the 1950s, but it was the cartoon series that brought it to a wider audience. What does it mean? Apparently, it was coined just for the sound of it as an exclamation by a character in the American children's TV programme *The Howdy Doody Show* in 1954.

Another surfers' slang term popularized by the Turtles was '**mondo**', meaning 'extremely' or 'very', as in 'This dude is mondo evil!' It was adopted from the title of an Italian film popular in the 1960s, *Mondo Cane* (literally 'World of a Dog').

Crackerjack!

Crackerjack

Crackerjack was shown on BBC1 from 1955 to 1984, always starting at 4.55 so that the show's opening announcement could remain the same: 'It's Friday ... it's five to five ... it's *Crackerjack*!' Behavioural psychologists might have taken more than a passing interest in this children's programme, for its title exerted an extraordinary power over the studio audience. Every time the name of the show was uttered by one of the cast, the audience would yell '**Crackerjack!**' in a response so well drilled it would have put Pavlov's dogs to shame.

After the formulaic beginning, accompanied by frenzied cheering from the audience of tartrazine-fuelled pre-teens, thirty minutes of comic mayhem ensued. At least it would in the 1970s. When the show kicked off in the 1950s it was a rather sedate affair, hosted by Eamonn Andrews and involving a desk-bound quiz with the infamous **Crackerjack pencils** as prizes. Later hosts included such luminaries as Michael Aspel and Leslie Crowther, but perhaps it is Ed 'Stewpot' Stewart's time at the helm that is most fondly recalled. The slapstick comedy of Don McLean, Peter Glaze and Jan Hunt was the highlight of the show during this era, although their singing exploits were also in evidence, as every week they would gamely cover a top-forty hit – such as David Bowie's 'Golden Years' – during the middle of the show's main sketch.

Crackerjack's cast changed again in the 1980s. Stu Francis became the presenter and The Krankies (see page 52) provided the komedy. The quiz element of the show remained, but instead of cabbages being dished out for wrong answers, as they were in the 1970s, failure was punished with the dropping of gunge from a great height. Noel Edmonds, evidently, was taking notes.

Stu Francis had a number of catchphrases – 'Oh, I could crush a grape', 'Oh, I could wrestle an Action Man!' and 'Oh, I could jump off a doll's house!' – none of which particularly captured the nation's imagination. Which just goes to show that although the power of television to influence the way we speak is great, it is not supernatural.

cushty

⇨ See **Only Fools and Horses**

Dad's Army

From 1968 to 1977, Britain re-fought World War II – but this time it was for laughs. Captain Mainwaring's Home Guard platoon vigilantly watched the coastline of the fictitious town of Walmington-on-Sea for a German invasion that ultimately never came. The ageing volunteers rarely saw any Germans, apart from some captured submariners, and spent most of their time trying to pull rank on a clergyman, his verger and a bolshie air-raid warden, all of whom had claims to the church hall in which Mainwaring's men drilled.

Dad's Army, written by David Croft and Jimmy Croft, was inspired by the latter's experiences in the Home Guard. It prolonged the careers of a number of veteran actors who, in return, provided comedy with perhaps more memorable characters than any other sitcom. The show had more than its fair share of memorable catchphrases too.

Captain Mainwaring (Arthur Lowe) was the platoon's leader. A rotund bank manager, he was an unlikely leader of fighting men and his pomposity earned him the nickname 'Napoleon' from the ARP warden. Mainwaring was educated at a grammar school, and the class tensions between him and his upper-class second-in-command, the unflappable and ever-polite Sergeant Wilson (John Le Mesurier) was a source of much of *Dad's Army*'s more subtle comedy.

Mainwaring was frequently exasperated by the foolish words and actions of Private Frank Pike (Ian Lavender), a mother's boy too young to fight in the regular army. When Pike's naivety irked the captain, Mainwaring's withering retort of '**Stupid boy**' would put the private in his place again.

Sharp-tongued undertaker Corporal Frazer (John Laurie) was a gloomy Caledonian presence in the ranks. An ex-sailor, his pessimism in difficult situations was expressed in the trademark cry of **'We're doomed!'**

Corporal Jones (Clive Dunn), a butcher since retiring as a career soldier, had many tales to tell of his time in uniform in Africa. He would recount these stories – most of which concerned 'fuzzy-wuzzies' and his decided opinion that **'They don't like it up 'em'** – at the drop of a hat, often interrupting Captain Mainwaring with **'Permission to speak, sir.'** An excitable old soldier, Jones often got into a flap when anything out of the ordinary happened. His interjection of **'Don't panic! Don't panic!'** was in stark contrast to his own less than calm behaviour.

All of these catchphrases have proved irresistible to the British public and have lasted long after the programme ended: people in authority still dismiss the hare-brained ideas of their juniors with 'Stupid boy'; any perilous situation is likely to give rise to shouts of 'Don't panic!' and 'We're doomed!'; while bullish sports commentators are apt to talk up the chances of British teams by noting that their supposedly less physical overseas opponents 'don't like it up 'em'.

Dad's Army also featured a memorable theme tune, **'Who do you think you are kidding, Mr Hitler?'**, which was recorded by entertainer Bud Flanagan shortly before he died. The title of this song is still very popular with newspaper sub-editors who like to use it in headlines about people, usually politicians, with whom they have a bone to pick. In April 2004, for example, some 27 years after the final episode was shown, the *Daily Mirror* invoked the memory of *Dad's Army* with this assault on the Prime Minister: 'Who do you think you are kidding, Mr Blair? Don't panic! Don't panic! Corporal Tony's taken charge! Britain is safe from the hordes of migrants who might have come here next week.'

Dalek

Doctor Who

Fans of the long-running series *Doctor Who* (see page 44) have seen their hero confront a huge number of enemies over the years, some of them more than once. The Master, an evil Time Lord, has been a thorn in the Doctor's side, as have the Cybermen. His most frequent adversaries, however, have been the **Daleks**.

The Daleks are a race of robots created from the mutated remains of a people called the Kaleds who lived on the planet Skaro. They were created by an evil wheelchair-bound scientist called Davros and have been terrorizing the universe for many years. The Daleks shoot first and ask questions later. Anyone who gives the incorrect response to their command of 'You will obey!' can expect a burst from a ray gun preceded by the frenzied – and much imitated – cry of '**Exterminate! Exterminate!**'

In terms of impact on culture, it can be argued that the Daleks have proved more popular than the Doctor himself. For example, the Doctor cannot be found in any dictionary, but the word 'Dalek' can. Terry Nation, who created the Daleks and based the design on a pepperpot, first claimed that the word derived from an encyclopdia volume that started at 'dal' and finished at 'lek'. He changed his story later on, though, and it seems he arrived at the word spontaneously. He was, however, pleased to discover in later years that *dalek* means 'far and distant thing' in Serbo-Croat.

The fact that Nation based the Daleks on the Nazis may, in a country still obsessed with World War II, explain the relentless robots' popularity. When the Daleks first appeared on *Doctor Who*, the public couldn't get enough of them. Merchandisers had a field day as Nation's creations were used to sell everything from soap to breakfast cereal. Dalekmania almost matched Beatlemania for a time, and there was even a hit single 'I'm Gonna Spend My Christmas with a Dalek' (released by The Go Gos in 1964).

The mechanical monsters have even been a source of comic inspiration. Victor Lewis-Smith gave us the gay Daleks, while a Pakistani Dalek was the distinctly un-PC creation of Spike Milligan. The Daleks were most memorably invoked by playwright Dennis Potter in 1993, when he compared BBC Director-General John Birt to a 'croak-voiced Dalek'. For many years after this comparison, the magazine *Private Eye* portrayed Birt as a Dalek in its cartoons.

Del Boy

⇨ See **Only Fools and Horses**

diddy

The Ken Dodd Show

The popularity of '**diddy**' as a somewhat derisory colloquial word meaning 'tiny' is due in no small part to buck-toothed, wild-haired comedy legend Ken Dodd, who introduced the world to the Diddymen in the 1960s as a regular feature of *The Ken Dodd Show*.

The Diddymen were an assortment of diminutive characters, including Dicky Mint, Hamish McDiddy and Nigel Ponsonby Smallpiece, who inhabited the fictional Diddyland, notionally located in the Liverpool suburb of Knotty Ash, and famous for its jam-butty mines. In some early performances, the Diddymen were portrayed on stage by children and midgets dressed in pantomime costumes and masks, but it was as puppets created by Roger Stevenson that their characters were fully realized. Indeed, they proved so popular that they later took centre stage in a children's show, *Ken Dodd and the Diddymen*, which ran for 28 episodes between 1969 and 1972.

The popularity of the Diddymen was such that the word 'diddy' (which is first recorded in the 1930s as a childish corruption of 'little') came to be widely used to suggest that something was so small that it belonged in the miniaturized world of Ken Dodd's puppet theatre. Many things have been categorized as 'diddy' in the subsequent years: flats, microcomputers, the Daewoo Matiz, and even Wimbledon Football Club's midfield quartet.

⇨ See also **marmalize**

Didn't she do well?
⇨ See **The Generation Game**

dipstick
Only Fools and Horses

The Chambers Dictionary offers two definitions of the word '**dipstick**'. It is 'a rod for measuring the depth of liquid in a sump, etc', and can also be a derogatory slang word meaning 'a stupid or foolish person'.

Television viewers were most likely to encounter the first sense of the word on *It's a Knockout* (see page 147), where the dipstick was the tool used by referee Arthur Ellis to measure the amounts of coloured liquid that teams managed to transport into containers after negotiating the show's elaborate obstacle courses.

The derogatory sense of the word was first heard by many British viewers in the American comedy caper *The Dukes of Hazzard*, broadcast between 1979 and 1985, where it was a favourite insult of Sheriff Rosco P Coltrane (played by James Best). The term was apparently employed as a sanitized version of the southern American term 'dipshit', and was frequently applied by Rosco to his hapless deputies Enos (Sonny Shroyer) and Cletus (Rick Hurst).

However, it is now most popularly associated with the show *Only Fools and Horses* (see page 142), where Del Boy Trotter bandies it about freely as an insult to his brother Rodney. It is now hard to hear the word 'dipstick' without thinking of David Jason's Del Boy character, although it has not quite reached the level of popularity of some of the show's other catchphrases. In a recent poll only 4% of the show's fans named it as

"In the middle of the worst winter for two million years — with the weathermen laying odds on a new Ice Age — this dipstick goes and buys out Amber Solaire!"

their favourite Del Boy catchphrase, whereas 'You plonker!' topped the poll with 19% of fans voting for it.

Dirty Den

EastEnders

The focal point of the BBC soap opera *EastEnders* (first screened in 1985) has always been the local pub 'The Queen Vic', and much of the show's early appeal came from the character of the pub's landlord, Dennis Watts. He was a smooth-talking blend of lady-killer and tough guy, whose behaviour was soon to make him a favourite of the tabloid press, where he was dubbed '**Dirty Den**'.

Den, played by Leslie Grantham, earned this label partly by being seen to be involved in all sorts of nefarious activities, but chiefly because of his frequent infidelity to his rather flaky and gullible wife Angie (played by Anita Dobson). Among his conquests was the teenage Michelle Fowler (Susan Tully) who bore him a child. The character's notoriety was accentuated in the public mind by the revelation that Grantham was in real life a convicted killer who had served time in prison.

On screen the love-rat's career seemed to come to a sudden end in 1989 with a gunshot and the splash of a body falling into the canal, but things were deliberately left less than totally clear. Fourteen years later, with the ratings in need of a boost, this favourite character was duly written back in with the story that he had faked his own death to avoid the attentions of vengeful gangsters. But Dirty Den's return was not a great success, and he was killed off a second time – presumably for good – in 2005.

Not only did the character's nickname become a byword for callous cruelty, but the pleasing alliteration provided a template for tabloid journalists. In subsequent years it has been echoed in headlines about other media hate figures, notably 'Nasty Nick' Bateman, a pariah from *Big Brother*, and 'Nasty Nigel' Lythgoe, a judge on the talent show *Popstars*.

Doctor Who

Few programmes have generated such a loyal – some might say obsessive – following as *Doctor Who*. Ever since it was axed by the BBC in 1989, the Whovians (as enthusiasts of the show call themselves) have campaigned tirelessly for the Doctor's return to a regular timeslot. In 2005 they got their wish, and the time-travelling hero reappeared on our screens in a new series starring Christopher Ecclestone.

Doctor Who is Britain's most celebrated home-grown science-fiction TV show and ranks alongside *Star Trek* in terms of cult status and influence on popular culture. Created by the BBC in 1963, it concerns the adventures of a mysterious man known only as 'The Doctor' who travels through space and time battling various villains and monsters.

In fact, the Doctor is not really a man at all, but rather a **Time Lord** from the planet Gallifrey. Time Lords are supposedly the most powerful race of beings in the universe, possessing the technology to travel in time and, therefore, the ability to shape or reshape the past, present and future. The Doctor's wanderlust means that he rarely returns to his home planet, preferring instead to roam the universe in search of adventure, usually in the company of attractive young female assistants.

One advantage of being a Time Lord is that the Doctor has twelve lives. When one life comes to an end he can 'regenerate' from one body into another. This is very handy for television executives, as it means that when one actor tires of saving the universe, he can be replaced by another. A total of nine actors have played the Doctor so far: William Hartnell (1963–6), Patrick Troughton (1966–9), Jon Pertwee (1970–4), Tom Baker

(1974–81), Peter Davison (1981–4), Colin Baker (1984–6), Sylvester McCoy (1987–9), Paul McGann (in a one-off special in 1996) and Christopher Ecclestone (2005), with David Tennant slated to become the tenth. But in spite of his Gallifreyan origins, throughout all of his incarnations the Doctor has been a peculiarly British character. Dressed eccentrically in clothes that call to mind the Victorian or Edwardian era, and using intelligence and charm rather than firepower to outwit his adversaries, the Doctor is vaguely reminiscent of Sherlock Holmes. Perhaps this Britishness explains the show's longevity.

It has to be said, however, that Sherlock Holmes never encountered such exotically named life forms as the Cybermen, the Zygons or the Vervoids. Nor did he need to master the workings of a time vector generator or a **sonic screwdriver**. This last gadget was introduced in 1968, and has become synonymous with sci-fi gadgetry. Capable of picking locks and repairing damaged equipment, it got the Doctor out of many a tight spot until it was destroyed in 1982 by a hostile alien. The writers came up with a sonic lance for the Doctor to use against the Cybermen in 1985, but this did not capture fans' imagination, and in his latest incarnations the Doctor and the sonic screwdriver have been reunited.

Doctor Who's two most enduring creations, however, have been the **Daleks** (see page 40) and the **Tardis** (see page 180). These have both proved so successful that the words have now been entered in some dictionaries, and the concepts they embody are widely understood even by people who have rarely seen the show.

D'oh!

⇨ See **The Simpsons**

Don't have nightmares

Crimewatch UK

Compared to many countries, Britain has a low crime rate. Many of its citizens will never experience any sort of crime, let alone a serious one. But some newspapers paint a different picture, portraying the UK as a lawless nation urgently in need of being taken in hand by a firm government. The plethora of crime-related programmes that currently dominate the TV schedules might have something to do with this perception. Among these is *Crimewatch UK*, a programme where the police request information from viewers to help them solve crimes.

Crimewatch has been running since 1984 and is based on the snappily titled German show *Aktenzeichen XY Ungelöst* (which translates as 'File XY Unsolved'). Its main presenter is Nick Ross, who has been hosting the show since the first programme. Each week, after numerous crimes have been either described or dramatically reconstructed, Ross reassures the audience that such misdeeds and outrages are statistically uncommon. He then tells viewers to sleep well and adds, **'Don't have nightmares.'**

Although the show is sometimes criticized for either frightening people or attracting viewers who get a kick out of violence, the BBC can point to *Crimewatch*'s invaluable help in the solving of hundreds of crimes, including over 50 murders. The programme's mercifully violence-free Aladdin's Cave feature has also succeeded in reuniting many owners with their antiques and other valuables.

Don't mention the war

Fawlty Towers

The attitude of many older Britons to World War II can perhaps best be summed up in the now legendary scene from 'The Germans', an episode of the sitcom *Fawlty Towers* (see page 66). In it, hotelier Basil Fawlty, befuddled by a blow to the head after a stuffed moose-head falls down on him, upsets a group of German guests by raking up memories of Germany's Nazi past. Despite having taken exaggerated pains beforehand to warn his staff '**Don't mention the war**', Basil ends up making reference to the Third Reich every time he opens his mouth, culminating in a frenzied goose-stepping march that invokes both *Monty Python*'s Ministry of Silly Walks and the Wehrmacht right in front of his astonished guests.

Prior to the maniacal march, there is a memorable exchange between Fawlty and one of the Germans, who pleads, 'Will you stop talking about the war!' Basil looks surprised and says, 'Me? You started it!' 'We did not start it!' retorts the guest. 'Yes, you did!' says Basil. 'You invaded Poland!'

The phrase 'Don't mention the war' has stuck firmly in the British imagination, and has come to embody the nation's often insensitive attitude to Germany. In 2005, when a member of Britain's royal family attended a fancy-dress party as a Nazi, *The Independent* could not resist alluding to the famous scene: 'Whatever you do, don't mention the war. Oops! Prince Harry joins a long list of miscreants responsible for anti-Germanic gaffes and other xenophobic clichés.'

Moreover, the phrase is not restricted to references to World War II. It was also co-opted by *The Guardian* when Tony Blair's government faced embarrassment over the 2003 conflict in Iraq: 'Don't mention the war: anger as Iraq is kept off Labour agenda.'

Don't panic! Don't panic!

⇨ See **Dad's Army**

Don't try this at home, kids!

⇨ See **Good thinking, Batman!**

early bath
Grandstand

When a sportsman is sent off from the field of play for violent conduct, does he really relax in the warm water of a large communal bath and wait for his mud-spattered colleagues to troop in at the final whistle? Whatever the reality, it is almost obligatory for commentators to refer to a dismissed player as going for an '**early bath**' as he trudges from the playing area to the boos of the opposing supporters.

The enduring nature of this expression is a testament to the influence of the legendary broadcaster Eddie Waring, who brightened up many a rainy Saturday afternoon in the 1960s and 1970s with his commentaries on rugby league as part of the BBC's flagship sports programme *Grandstand*. Rugby league matches were a staple of *Grandstand* from its inception in 1958, and Waring, who had been an innovative manager in the 1930s and had in the post-war years established himself as the sport's premier journalist, was a natural choice to provide the commentary. He soon made the sport popular far beyond its traditional heartland in the north of England.

It is said that he developed some of his more colourful terminology as a means of entertaining the viewers when players became so covered in mud that it was impossible to identify them. Besides 'early bath' he is also remembered for his cry of '**up-and-under**' whenever a player hoisted a high kick up over the onrushing defence and ran under it in an attempt to recover the ball as it fell.

Waring's distinctive delivery – he somehow managed to pronounce 'rugby' as though it contained four syllables: 'ah-rug-a-bee' – made him a gift to impressionists, and he was a favourite subject for Mike Yarwood, television's leading mimic of the time. This exposure further helped to establish his catchphrases in the public mind.

Besides his regular gig as a rugby league commentator, Eddie Waring also co-presented *It's a Knockout* and made memorable guest appearances on *The Morecambe and Wise Show* and *The Goodies*. He finally hung up his microphone in 1981 to be replaced by the worthy but comparatively dour Ray French.

early doors

ITV Sport

The phrase '**early doors**' has become familiar as a way of referring to the opening phase of some activity. It is especially associated with football commentary, as in: 'You don't want to concede a goal early doors or you'll have a mountain to climb, Brian.'

Many people associate the phrase with the pundit Ron Atkinson, believing it to have emerged fully formed from his bizarrely coiffured head, along with other items of 'Ronglish' such as 'crowd scene' (when there are a lot of players in the penalty area), 'back stick' (the goalpost on the far side of the pitch from the player with the ball) and 'spotter's badge' (a notional award given to a player who demonstrates good awareness of colleagues' positions).

Atkinson, a former player and manager, was a regular member of ITV Sport's commentary team for televised football matches in the 1990s and 2000s, adding his expert thoughts to the commentaries of Brian Moore and Clive Tyldesley, until being sacked after making an offensive comment on air in 2004.

Although Big Ron is widely credited with popularizing the saying 'early doors', the phrase may in fact have its origins in American show-business slang, where the 'door' is the attendance at a performance, and the 'early door' refers to the number of people turning up at an early stage of the evening, before the main attraction goes onstage.

Eat my shorts!

⇨ See **The Simpsons**

ecky thump

The Goodies

In March 1975, Britain was in the grip of a martial arts craze. It had started with the films of Bruce Lee, but now everyone seemed to be cashing in on the phenomenon: Carl Douglas had topped the charts the previous December with 'Kung Fu Fighting', and the cartoon show *Hong Kong Phooey* was established as a children's-hour favourite. It was high time for someone to send the whole thing up, and no 1970s television programme was better equipped for the job than *The Goodies*, which obliged gloriously with a tale of the ancient Lancastrian martial art of **ecky thump**.

The Goodies were a three-man comedy team who graduated from the Cambridge Footlights in the early 1960s. They had considered and rejected the titles *Super-Chaps Three* and *Narrow Your Mind* for their surreal comedy show before finally settling on *The Goodies*. Under this name, the programme ran for 73 episodes between 1970 and 1981. The format involved the team members playing caricatured versions of themselves: Tim Brooke-Taylor appeared as a patriotic upper-class twit, Graeme Garden as a manic inventor, and Bill Oddie as a north-country beatnik. This ill-assorted trio advertised 'We do anything, anytime, anywhere', which was a convenient starting point for a variety of improbable adventures to which they travelled on a distinctive three-seater bike.

The episode that introduced the world to ecky thump was entitled 'Kung Fu Kapers' and was first broadcast on 24 March 1975. In this episode, Tim and Graeme's attempts to take up kung fu were put into the shade as Bill revealed himself to be a master of ecky thump, an ancient Lancastrian art whose practitioners inflict damage by skilfully wielding black puddings. For months afterwards, children would shout 'ecky thump!' as they aimed karate chops at each other in school playgrounds up and down the land.

The episode had another unforeseen side-effect. While watching with his wife, a viewer in Norfolk thought the spoof was so funny that he fell into a fit of hysterical laughter which continued for half an hour, after which he succumbed to a fatal heart attack. His widow made a point of writing to the Goodies to thank them for making the final minutes of her husband's life so happy.

Eh-oh

⇨ See **Big hug!**

Evenin' all

Dixon of Dock Green

Despite corruption scandals and allegations of institutional racism, the British police force is still held up by many as the finest and most honest in the world. This wholesome reputation has been promoted by TV images of the British bobby on the beat, and none more so than that of George Dixon in *Dixon of Dock Green*, which was a staple of British television from 1955 right up to 1976. Created by Ted Willis, the show ran for a total of 367 episodes.

PC (from 1964 Sergeant) Dixon, who was played by Jack Warner, would bookend each episode, beginning with the greeting '**Evenin' all**' and ending with some wise words to camera drawing a moral message from the story just played out, before signing off with a reassuring smile and a sharp salute. Warner had first played the role in the 1949 film *The Blue Lamp*, in which he was shot dead by a character played by Dirk Bogarde. However, Jack Warner defied not only the grim reaper but also the police youth policy to reprise the role on television: he was already 60 when the show started and well past retirement age when its run ended. In later years, he played a less and less active role in the storyline (not least because he suffered from arthritis), but he would always be there at the start and end of each episode to make viewers feel that they could sleep safely in their beds. Such was the respect in which he and the show were held that, when he died in 1981, his coffin was carried by officers from Paddington Green police station.

His name and catchphrase are often evoked as emblematic of a golden age when a policeman was your best friend and young tearaways could be put in their place by a firm word and a stern look. The contrast with the more violent, gritty and action-packed *The Sweeney* (see page 192), which began in the year George Dixon signed off for the last time, could not be greater.

Exterminate! Exterminate!

⇨ See **Dalek**

FAB

⇨ See **Thunderbirds are go!**

Fandabidozi!

The Krankies Klub

Scotland has given the world comics of the stature of Chic Murray, Stanley Baxter and Billy Connolly, but in the 1970s it blotted its copybook somewhat when it produced The Krankies. This husband-and-wife duo (real names Ian and Janette Tough) provided music-hall mirth for a mainly youthful audience on shows such as *Crackerjack, The Krankies Klub*, and *The Krankies Elektronik Komic*. Jimmy Krankie (Janette dressed as a schoolboy) played it for laughs while Ian was the straight man in a double act that provided the English language with a word to express untrammelled approbation. Whenever Wee Jimmy wished to emote delight he would give a double thumbs-up followed by the exclamation '**Fandabidozi!**' Occasionally, his joy was so unconfined that only 'Fandabi-double-dozi!' would do.

The Krankies were at their peak in 1980s, when they were a fixture on television and even released a single (unsurprisingly called 'Fandabidozi'). Although they eventually fell out of favour on television, the kream of Kaledonian komedy did make a brief reappearance on the small screen in the 1990s, in a pastiche of *The Silence of the Lambs* written by and starring Dawn French and Jennifer Saunders.

The word 'fandabidozi' is still sometimes used – mainly ironically – by Britons of a certain vintage. A recent outing was in the British gangster film *Sexy Beast* (2000), when a retired villain (played by Ray Winstone) delighted viewers by using 'fandabidozi' to describe a scorching-hot day on the Costa del Sol.

feck

⇨ See **Go on, go on, go on, go on, go on, go on**

Flobbadob!

The Flowerpot Men

Complaints that the low educational content of children's television was impairing infant language development did not start with the *Teletubbies* (see page 16). In the earliest days of children's broadcasting, there was a similar storm of protest over 'Oddle-Poddle', a childish language whose most memorable utterance was the word '**Flobbadob!**' (or its more rococo variant '**Flobbalobbalob!**').

'Oddle-Poddle' was the incomprehensible tongue spoken by Bill and Ben, two string puppets with bodies made of flowerpots who featured in *The Flowerpot Men*, a programme which was first shown as part of BBC's *Watch with Mother* in 1952. The two puppets had their names painted on their backs, but were otherwise identical, except that Bill spoke in falsetto, while Ben had a sombre, deep voice (both provided by Peter Hawkins). The pair lived in two large flowerpots at the bottom of a garden, and would emerge to get up to mischief as soon as the gardener went indoors for dinner. Little Weed (who was even less articulate – her only utterance was 'Weeeeeed!'), a large sunflower between their pots, kept lookout for them, and there was a calling to account at the end of each episode, with the vital question 'Was it Bill or was it Ben?' being posed to identify the chief transgressor.

The origins of Bill and Ben's peculiar language in fact lie in three stories broadcast on the BBC radio series *Listen with Mother* in 1951. Written by Hilda Brabben, they were based on stories she told to her much younger brothers William and Benjamin, who contributed more than their names to the show. Apparently 'Flobbadob' was what they said when one of the pair broke wind in the bath – not a piece of information the BBC would have been keen to publicize in the genteel 1950s.

Twenty-six episodes of the series were made by 1954, with scripts by Freda Lingstrom, and these were repeated over the next two decades. The characters were revived in 2001, using stop-motion animation and foam-and-wire puppets (the originals being long-term inmates of the Museum of London), for a further 52 episodes. The revived Flowerpot Men proved quite popular, and even released a single ('Flobbadance') in 2002.

Friends

'Most viewers felt the show was not very entertaining, clever or original ... Stated viewing intentions for a series based on this pilot were not encouraging.'

So said NBC's secret verdict on the 1994 pilot show of a new sitcom called *Friends*. From this unpromising start, the show about six New York singletons became one of the most popular and successful television programmes of all time, influencing drinking habits, hairstyles and even the English language during its ten-year run.

The show revolved around six attractive young residents of the Big Apple. In the first series, Rachel Green (Jennifer Aniston) is a spoilt rich kid forced to work as a waitress while trying to break into the world of fashion. Her flatmate Monica Geller (Courteney Cox) is a chef with an obsession for neatness. Monica's brother Ross (David Schwimmer) is a neurotic palaeontologist whose wife has just left him for another woman. Across the hall from Monica and Rachel live an aspiring actor called Joey Tribbiani (Matt LeBlanc) and a wisecracking data processor called Chandler Bing (Matthew Perry) who is an old college friend of Ross. The sextet is completed by Phoebe Buffay (Lisa Kudrow), a masseuse and the most eccentric of the lead characters.

The characters undergo various changes of role and fortune over the next ten years – notably Monica and Chandler get married to each other, while Ross and Rachel conduct an off-and-on romance – but the six continue to provide a tight-knit mutual support group that most viewers can only envy.

The friends are often seen hogging the big couch in their favourite coffee shop, Central Perk, and sipping a latte or two. Before *Friends* and *Frasier* (another sitcom where a coffee shop was a regular backdrop), establishments in Britain serving proper coffee were a rarity. Now, in part thanks to these two shows, they are ubiquitous and many boast large comfy couches that are consciously styled on the one in Central Perk.

Another notable effect *Friends* had was in the world of hairdressing. For many women, Jennifer Aniston's hair was to die for. The hairstyle she wore in the first few series of the show became immensely popular and inspired thousands of women to ask for a '**Rachel cut**'. This style, which was created by Chris McMillan, involved the hair being layered to frame the cheeks and became *the* look of the 1990s.

Friends may have been hugely influential in terms of setting lifestyle trends, but the show's effect on the English of young Britons is less certain. *Friends* was just the most notable of many imported programmes that helped to popularize a distinctive type of youth speech on this side of the Atlantic. As with the Australian speech patterns of *Neighbours* (see page 136), sentences tend to end on an upward tone that make statements sound like questions. Other characteristics are the use of the word '**like**' when reporting speech (see page 93), the employment of '**so**' as an intensifying word in grammatically unorthodox places (see page 167) and the frequent use of the exclamation '**Oh my God!**' – taken to extraordinary lengths by Chandler's ex-girlfriend Janice (Maggie Wheeler), who manages to draw it out into three distinct sentences: 'Oh. My. God.'

Typical of the style is Phoebe's opening monologue at the start of the second series: 'OK, so this is pretty much what's happened so far. Ross was in love with Rachel since, you know, forever, but every time he tried to tell her, something kind of got in the way, like cats, and Italian guys. Finally Chandler was like "Forget about her", but when Ross was in China on his dig, Chandler let it slip that Ross was in love with Rachel. She was like "Oh my God!" So she went to the airport to meet him when he came back, but what she didn't know was that Ross was getting off the plane with another woman. Uh-oh! So, that's pretty much everything you need to know. But, enough about us. So, how've you been?'

Besides helping to influence the general manner of speaking among young people, the show also helped to popularize certain specific phrases. Devotees of *Friends* learned that 'to be there for someone' meant to provide support at a time of difficulty, while there was a long-running gag around being 'on a break', which referred to being at a point in a relationship when it is permissible to date other people. Of wider linguistic application were the phrase '**go commando**' (see page 59) and the chat-up line '**How you doin'?**' (see page 70).

Fuhgedaboudit

⇨ See **The Sopranos**

funny old game
Saint and Greavsie

Jimmy Greaves knows about the ups and downs of football more than most. A prolific scorer for Tottenham and England, he looked set to crown his playing career with a World Cup winner's medal in 1966. However, a leg injury in one of the tournament's earlier matches meant that he was replaced by Geoff Hurst, whose form kept a desperately frustrated Greaves out of the team for the rest of England's victorious run. When the home side defeated West Germany in the final, Greaves was the only Englishman in Wembley not beside himself with joy. As the exhausted but delighted England players held up the Jules Rimet Trophy, Greaves watched from the sidelines, perhaps musing that football was a **funny old game**.

'It's a funny old game' is a maxim often used to describe a sport, particularly football, when something unexpected happens. Perhaps he did not coin it, but Jimmy Greaves is the person most associated with the phrase, owing to his frequent use of it in his role as a football pundit on ITV throughout the 1980s and into the 1990s. He teamed up with former Liverpool and Scotland striker Ian St John, first on *World of Sport* and then, from 1985, on their own show called *Saint and Greavsie*. Their programme, in which goals from the previous week's games were combined with anecdotes and banter (usually about the ineptitude of Scottish goalkeepers), ran for a number of years. After it ended the duo released a compilation video called *Saint and Greavsie's 'It's a Funny Old Game'*. This was the genesis of the football comedy video, a genre which has given us such gems as *Alan Hansen's 'High, Wide and Hansen'*, *Emlyn Hughes presents 'My Gran Could Do Better'* and *Richard Littlejohn's 'We Woz Robbed'*.

Get down, Shep!

Blue Peter

The children's TV programme *Blue Peter* (see page 18) is often remembered for featuring an incontinent elephant, but Lulu was not the only animal made famous by this show. Indeed, throughout its history the show's presenters have been accompanied by various pets. Maggie and Jim, the tortoises, joined the show in 1979 and were named after Mrs Thatcher and Mr Callaghan, two politicians then competing for occupancy of Number 10 Downing Street.

Tortoises, it has to be said, are not very exciting, and so it is the *Blue Peter* dogs that are best remembered, and in particular John Noakes's dog, Shep. For a number of years Shep was a constant companion of Noakes, accompanying him on outside broadcasts and sitting well-behaved at his feet in the studio. At least, that was the plan. All too often, the excitable Border collie would leap up and put John off what he was saying, earning the playful pooch the admonition '**Get down, Shep!**'

Such was the frequency of Shep's interruptions that John's exasperated command became an unintended catchphrase. For a while, Noakes's cry became widely imitated for comedy purposes and those masters of the novelty record The Barron Knights even released a top-forty single called 'Get Down, Shep!'

Give us a twirl

⇨ See **The Generation Game**

57

Gizza job

Boys from the Blackstuff

Rare is the programme that can not only entertain and educate its viewers but capture the national mood as well. One such programme, *Boys from the Blackstuff*, managed that feat in 1982. *Blackstuff*'s stark catchphrase '**Gizza job**' neatly summed up recession-hit Britain and was a perfect riposte to Norman Tebbit's unsympathetic injunction to the jobless to 'get on their bikes' and look for work.

Boys from the Blackstuff, a five-part drama, was first shown on BBC2 in the autumn of 1982. Written by Liverpudlian Alan Bleasdale, it depicted the lives of five unemployed tarmac layers in the writer's home city. Effectively a sequel to Bleasdale's *Black Stuff*, a one-off *Play for Today* shown in 1980, it won a number of awards for its uncompromising dissection of the effects of long-term unemployment on working-class men and their families. The most memorable character in the series was Yosser Hughes, played by Bernard Hill. Hughes, anxious to keep his family together, pleads for employment of any sort with increasingly desperate cries of '**Gizza job**' and '**I could do that**', but no-one can help him. He eventually suffers a mental collapse and his children are taken into care.

Boys from the Blackstuff won instant acclaim and was quickly transferred to BBC1 where it found an even bigger audience and still more plaudits. The programme's two catchphrases also quickly entered into the nation's consciousness and are still an instant reminder of a particularly bleak period in Britain's post-war history.

go commando

Friends

The phrase 'to **go commando**', meaning to dispense with the use of underpants, was a relatively obscure item of American college slang before it was popularized by an episode of the situation comedy *Friends* (see page 54).

The expression is recorded in *Cassell's Dictionary of Slang* as originating in the 1970s. Its derivation is unclear, but presumably there is a suggestion that soldiers on manoeuvres have no need for such luxuries as underwear.

The term might have remained the preserve of a clique of American students but for an episode of *Friends* called 'The One Where No-one's Ready', broadcast in 1996. This episode centres around Ross's exasperation at trying to get his friends organized to go out for a formal dinner. At one point, Joey explains that he needs to borrow some underwear because he is not currently wearing any, but he does not wish to 'go commando' when he changes into a rented tuxedo.

This single use of the phrase appealed to many British viewers, and the expression is now quite widely used. It often carries a hint of sexual titillation, but there can also be a suggestion of slovenliness, as when a person is forced to 'go commando' because they have forgotten to bring a spare pair of briefs to change into after taking strenuous exercise.

good game, good game

⇨ See **The Generation Game**

Good thinking, Batman!

Batman

If you make a well-intentioned suggestion (especially if your tone has a boy-scout earnestness to it), you might well receive the comment **'Good thinking, Batman!'** in reply. Whether this is a derisive put-down or an amused acknowledgement of thanks will be up to you to decide.

The character of Batman started life in a comic strip created by a 19-year-old called Bob Kane in 1939. It was brought to television by ABC in 1966 and the *Batman* show ran for 120 episodes over two years. The series was, at its peak, one of the most successful in US television history. Adults enjoyed its tongue-in-cheek humour, while children were enthralled by its cliff-hanging climaxes. The stars, however, played their roles in deadly earnest: Adam West's Batman was supported by Bruce Ward as his faithful sidekick Robin. 'Good thinking, Batman!' and other approving interjections were a staple of Ward's side of what a contemporary critic called the show's 'mahogany dialogue'.

Robin also had a penchant for coining exclamations of surprise using the formula **'Holy ..., Batman!'** Indeed, one anorak has painstakingly counted 352 separate variations on this theme, all the way from 'Holy Agility, Batman!' to 'Holy Zorro, Batman!'

The Dynamic Duo fought many villains, among the most memorable being the Riddler (Frank Gorshin), the Joker (Cesar Romero), the Penguin (Burgess Meredith) and Catwoman (played by several actresses, including Eartha Kitt). But no matter how evil the foe, nobody was ever killed, although there were fights aplenty, accompanied by comic-book screen-bursts of 'Wham!', 'Kapow!' and 'Sock!', all a little reminiscent of contemporary Pop Art.

When not engaged in physical combat, the pair were often seen performing gravity-defying vertical 'bat climbs' or speeding to and from their Batcave in their customized Batmobile.

Given all the breathless antics of the heroic pair, it was felt that impressionable children might copy some of the more dangerous stunts, so Batman would appear at the end of shows to warn them against such folly. This may even be the origin of the now proverbial phrase **'Don't try this at home, kids!'**

Go on, go on, go on, go on, go on, go on
Father Ted

A sitcom about three eccentric priests living with their equally strange housekeeper on a windswept island off the coast of Ireland does not sound like a recipe for comic gold. Yet in three series from 1995 to 1998, Graham Linehan and Arthur Matthews' creation *Father Ted* became immensely popular and is easily Channel 4's most successful home-grown sitcom. Its characters quickly entered into the public's consciousness, so much so that in 2000 Britain's Inland Revenue hired actress Pauline McLynn to reprise her role as housekeeper Mrs Doyle as the centrepiece of a high-profile advertising campaign.

In *Father Ted*, the catchphrase '**Go on, go on, go on, go on, go on, go on**' was employed most often when the dotty housekeeper tried to get someone to take a cup of tea or a sandwich. Such an attempt would start politely with 'Ah, go on', but if the offer was declined she would continue remorselessly, repeating the words over and over and over again until the reticent guest caved in.

In the hands of the Inland Revenue, Mrs Doyle's catchphrase became a tool to encourage people to fill in their tax returns promptly – and it worked. The number of forms received went up, and in January 2002 a spokeswoman said, 'Mrs Doyle has been quite a contributing factor. She's actually done her job.'

Mrs Doyle is one of the four main characters in *Father Ted*. The others are Father Jack (Frank Kelly), Father Dougal (Ardal O'Hanlan) and Father Ted himself (Dermot Morgan). The four live on Craggy Island in an unreal and surreal world where strange behaviour is commonplace and people think nothing of priests entering the Eurovision Song Contest. Father Ted is the most normal, although he is often driven to extreme acts and statements by his two colleagues. Dougal is a simple-minded soul who often seems to be operating on a completely different mental plane, while Jack is a whisky-soaked old lech who interacts with the world through profanities and violence alone. Appearing to suffer from Tourette's syndrome, he thunders out words at random such as '**feck**', 'arse', 'drink', and 'girls' when not sitting motionless in an alcoholic daze. 'Feck', of course, is a euphemistic deformation of another similar-sounding F-word, and was used with great relish by the cast and later copied by many of the show's fans.

guys and gals

⇨ See **How's about that then?**

Harry Enfield's Television Programme

Having achieved fame with his Loadsamoney character (see page 94), Harry Enfield moved swiftly from Channel 4 to his own show, *Harry Enfield's Television Programme*, which began on BBC2 in 1990. Aided and abetted by Paul Whitehouse and Kathy Burke, Enfield created some of the most popular comic characters of the next decade, many of whom had catchphrases which caught on in the nation's playgrounds and workplaces.

After two successful series of this character-based sketch show, Enfield moved to the larger stage of BBC1 in 1994 and produced a further two series. Although the show now had a new title – *Harry Enfield and Chums* – the format and most of the cast and characters remained the same.

These recurring characters included Wayne and Waynetta Slob, a council-housed couple of extraordinary laziness whose flat was a mess of dirty dishes, discarded pizza boxes, empty bottles and cigarette packets; the Old Gits, two astonishingly mean and selfish pensioners whose sole source of delight was observing other people's misfortunes; Kevin the teenager, a sullen and moody adolescent; and the narcissistic disc jockeys Mike Smash and Dave Nice, an uncannily accurate satire that perhaps sparked the revolution at Radio 1 in which the likes of Simon Bates and Dave Lee Travis were axed to make way for a younger generation.

A couple of the regular characters have come to represent certain social or historical types: Tim Nice-But-Dim became a paradigm for wealthy but feckless ex-public-schoolboys, while Mr Cholmondley-Warner exemplified the rather stilted patrician men who appeared in newsreels in the 1930s and 1940s, and the clipped form of English that they spoke.

Most of Enfield's characters had instantly recognizable catchphrases: Wayne and Waynetta Slob would explain to each other that they were far too busy to do whatever the other wanted because 'I am smoking a fag', while Kevin the teenager always responded to his long-suffering parents' entirely reasonable requests with a resentful 'That is so unfair!'

Perhaps the most widely imitated catchphrase from the show was provided by an elderly know-it-all wearing a white cap, who always announced his presence with an ear-piercing cry of 'Only me!' before interrupting someone in the middle of an activity. He would then barge in and offer unwanted advice, and when things went wrong he would deliver a chastening '**You don't want to do that!**' This catchphrase is still facetiously used as a commentary when someone pursues an ill-advised course of action.

Also widely copied were the Scousers, three quarrelsome Liverpudlians clad in shellsuits and sporting perms and moustaches. Easily riled, two of them would frequently come to blows and have to be separated by the third with a placatory '**Calm down! Calm down!**', only for the third party to become embroiled himself a short time later. People still copy this catchphrase – complete with the requisite Scouse accent – when they are seeking a light-hearted way to defuse a tense situation.

Hawk–Eye®

⇨ See **Snickometer**®

H-e-e-e-r-e's Johnny!
The Tonight Show

Depending on who you are, the words '**H-e-e-e-r-e's Johnny!**' will either conjure up a well-loved comedian and TV host or a murderous psychopath attempting to slay his family.

The words were first used to herald the nightly arrival of Johnny Carson, host of NBC's *The Tonight Show* from 1962 to 1992. Announcer Ed McMahon voiced the introduction as Carson arrived on stage to link sketches, interviews and music for a late-night audience. After taking over the show from Jack Paar, Carson became an American institution, and during his tenure the programme was often referred to as 'The Johnny Carson Show' or simply 'Carson'. McMahon's introduction became closely identified with the star, and his home town of Norfolk, Nebraska, now welcomes tourists with a billboard declaring, 'H-e-e-e-r-e's Norfolk, Proud Home Town of Johnny Carson'.

For those unfamiliar with American chat shows, however, 'H-e-e-e-r-e's Johnny!' has an altogether different meaning. In the 1980 film *The Shining*, the words and McMahon's distinctively drawn-out intonation are borrowed by a maniacally grinning Jack Nicholson as he smashes down the door of a room with an axe in order to do away with his wife, who is cowering in the corner. The scene, from Stanley Kubrick's cinematic interpretation of Stephen King's novel, is one of cinema's most unforgettable moments and has been reproduced many times on posters and T-shirts.

Hello, good evening and welcome
The Frost Report

During the 1970s, David Frost was a popular target for impressionists. An effective Frost impression did not require a long monologue, however. Indeed, all that was needed for a few laughs was a series of facial contortions while enunciating an elaborately elongated '**Hello, good evening and welcome**'.

This is a greeting that Frost has made his own in a number of programmes for both the BBC and ITV, initially as the ringmaster of the satirical *The Frost Report* (which built on the success he had achieved earlier with *That Was The Week That Was*), and then when he switched careers to become a heavyweight political interviewer, noted for his interrogations of the likes of Richard Nixon and the Shah of Iran.

Frost may have finished with satire after the 1960s, but satire had not finished with him: *Private Eye* regularly took him to task, while Peter Cook maintained that his one regret in life was saving Frost from drowning. Notwithstanding these attacks, Frost's career on both sides of the Atlantic followed an upward curve, as evidenced by his status as one of Concorde's first frequent flyers.

When he became a pioneer of breakfast television in the 1980s, Frost had to modify his catchphrase, changing 'evening' to 'morning'. Nevertheless, he remains a target for impressionists and satirists, although his once combative interviewing technique has been replaced by a more genial – some would say sycophantic – style.

Here's one I made earlier
⇨ See **Blue Peter**

her indoors

⇨ See **Arthur Daley**

He's from Barcelona
Fawlty Towers

Fawlty Towers is one of the world's best-loved sitcoms. Although only twelve episodes were made, between 1975 and 1979, the farcical goings-on at Torquay's worst hotel have become forever etched in the memory of the millions who watched the show. The comedy was based on the real experiences of John Cleese and other members of the *Monty Python* team who stayed at the Gleneagles Hotel in Torquay in 1971. The Pythons were not impressed by the standard of service nor by the ill-tempered manager.

Four years later those experiences were turned into a comedy penned by Cleese and his then wife Connie Booth. Cleese also took the lead role in the series as hotelier Basil Fawlty, a snobbish man with a short fuse who does not enjoy his job one bit. His lack of tact and frustrated ambitions are all too apparent, as is his dislike for his wife, Sybil (Prunella Scales). But the feeling is mutual, and Basil is often the victim of his wife's sharp tongue.

Sybil treats Basil badly, but Basil himself treats the hotel's staff appallingly, particularly Manuel (Andrew Sachs). Manuel is a Spanish waiter who is eager to please, but whose poor grasp of English exasperates Basil so much that minor mistakes are often punished with violence. Sybil is more tolerant of Manuel, explaining to guests **'He's from Barcelona'** whenever Manuel makes a slip-up. When the show was translated into Spanish, this line had to be changed and as far as most Spanish fans of *Fawlty Towers* are concerned, Manuel is Mexican (although for Basque viewers he is an Italian).

⇨ See also **Don't mention the war**

Hey!
Happy Days

Some television characters can be evoked by a single phrase, some memorable creations by a single word, but it is a rare character indeed that is brought to mind by a single syllable. One character who did manage this feat was Arthur Fonzarelli, known to his friends simply as 'The Fonz' or 'Fonzie', who set the standard for cool behaviour in the long-running American sitcom *Happy Days*.

Happy Days started out in 1974 as a traditional family sitcom, set in the 1950s, based around the central character of teenager Richie Cunningham (played by Ron Howard). However, it was the Cunningham family's lodger, the ultra-cool mechanic Fonzie (played by Henry Winkler) who stole the show. Fonzie cut an instantly recognizable figure in his leather jacket, white T-shirt and blue jeans, sporting an immaculate 'DA' haircut and constantly surrounded by admiring girls. He was also notable for his extremely economical use of language: a mere snap of his fingers was enough to summon the nearest pretty girl or get a troublesome piece of machinery to work; and as far as expressing emotions was concerned, most situations could be covered by raising both thumbs and saying '**Hey!**'

Fonzie continued to display effortless cool for a total of 256 episodes over ten years. By the time *Happy Days* ended in 1984 it had generated several spin-off programmes (including *Laverne and Shirley* and *Mork and Mindy*) and sent sales of leather jackets through the roof. It also had the rather unfortunate side-effect that teenage boys worldwide got hold of the idea that they too could look cool and pick up girls if only they raised their thumbs and said 'Hey!'

⇨ See also **correctamundo**

Hi-de-hi!

Hi-de-Hi!

The title of the successful BBC sitcom *Hi-de-Hi!* was taken from the rallying call at the fictional Maplin's holiday camp, broadcast over the PA system by indefatigable sports organizer and chief yellowcoat Gladys Pugh (Ruth Madoc). The campers' response was an initially enthusiastic but progressively more weary 'Ho-de-ho!' From this, '**Hi-de-hi!**' became a catchphrase summing up people's grim reaction to regimented entertainment and relentlessly programmed fun in all situations.

Hi-de-Hi! was a period piece, set in a typical British holiday camp of the late 1950s. The show's pilot episode was transmitted on New Year's Day, 1980, and a total of 57 episodes were broadcast before it eventually ended its run in 1988. Writers Jimmy Perry and David Croft drew on their own experiences when writing the series: Perry had been a Butlin's redcoat, and Croft an actor/producer of summer shows for a holiday camp. It was no accident that the name 'Maplin's' has the same number of letters and an entire syllable in common with 'Butlin's' and 'Pontin's'.

The storylines in *Hi-de-Hi!* revolved around a new entertainments manager Jeffrey Fairbrother (played by Simon Cadell), a well-meaning but hopeless academic, with whom the passionate and ambitious Gladys Pugh is hopelessly in love. Fairbrother's team of entertainers included bluff, beer-guzzling working-class comedian Ted Bovis (Paul Shane) and his hapless sidekick Spike Dixon (Jeffrey Holland). After initial personality clashes, the entertainers realize that they are all on the same side and that they face far greater challenges from the holiday-makers than from each other.

The call and response phrases 'hi-de-hi-de-hi-de-hi' and 'ho-de-ho-de-ho-de-ho' were originally used by American band leader and scat singer Cab Calloway in the 1940s, and are perhaps most familiar nowadays from his song 'Minnie the Moocher'. Legend has it that once he forgot the words during this particular number and improvised, the result being so successful that it became a staple of his act from then on.

Holy ..., Batman!

⇨ See **Good thinking, Batman!**

How's about that, then?

Jim'll Fix It

Dressed in trademark brightly coloured tracksuits and gold jewellery, Jimmy Savile has been part of the TV furniture for many years. His clothes, his shock of bleached hair and his penchant for large cigars make him an easy target for impressionists, as do his catchphrases such as '**How's about that, then?**'

This phrase and the other Savilisms, '**guys and gals**' and '**now then, now then**', don't really mean very much and are used by Sir Jim merely to use up dead time while he thinks about the next thing he wants to say. The phrases have been used countless times by Savile as a DJ on Radio 1 and *Top of the Pops* and, most memorably, on *Jim'll Fix It*.

Jim'll Fix It, which ran on BBC1 from 1973 to 1989, was based around a simple idea. Viewers, usually children, wrote in and asked Jim to make their dream come true. Whether it was driving in a James Bond car, singing with the Nottingham Forest squad, or having one's orchestral composition conducted by Edward Heath, Sir Jimmy made the dream come true and then presented the lucky viewer with a *Jim'll Fix It* badge.

Memorable 'fix its' included a patrol of cub scouts messily eating their lunch while enjoying a rollercoaster ride and a ten-year-old boy tagging with Big Daddy in a wrestling match. This was not Sir Jimmy's only experience in a wrestling ring. In the 1960s he wrestled professionally for a number of years at venues in the north of England. He was a star attraction for grapple fans, and maintains that 106 of his 107 bouts were sell-outs. His only fight without a full house, he claims, was due to a bus strike in Huddersfield.

How you doin'?

Friends

More pedantic viewers of the American sitcom *Friends* (see page 54) might wonder what the character of Joey is doing hanging around in a coffee bar with a bunch of geeky college-educated types. Joey himself is an often-out-of-work actor who is clearly not in the same intellectual league as palaeontologist Ross and data processor Chandler, nor does he have any reason to share their angst about conducting relationships with members of the opposite sex.

Joey may never have read a book that didn't have pictures, but he rarely has any difficulties getting to meet girls, especially when he uses his favourite chat-up line '**How you doin'?**', which he always pronounces with a heavy stress on the word 'you'.

There is nothing particularly sophisticated about the line, but it always works. Indeed, the fact that Joey's line is so lame, but at the same time so successful, whereas the droll Chandler usually flounders in his dealings with women, is the whole point of the joke.

Joey's chat-up line has become very popular with fans of the show and it now appears as a slogan on T-shirts, baseball caps and other merchandise. It has even survived into a post-*Friends* spin-off series, simply called *Joey*, that started in 2005, in which Matt LeBlanc's character finds himself transplanted to Hollywood.

> JOEY: Hey, Rach, how you doin'?
> RACHEL: I'm doin' good, baby. How you doin'?
> JOEY: Ross, don't let her drink any more!

I am not a number, I am a free man!

The Prisoner

An anonymous British secret agent, played by Patrick McGoohan, resigns his post following an angry confrontation with his boss. He drives home and prepares for a trip abroad, but while he packs, sleeping gas is released into his room and he falls unconscious. The next thing he knows he is in a place called The Village, talking to someone who identifies himself as 'Number 2' and who tells him that he is 'Number 6', to which McGoohan's character famously responds, '**I am not a number, I am a free man!**', a line that has subsequently come to stand for the indefatigable human spirit struggling to overcome the sinister forces that seek to oppress it.

Consisting of 17 episodes made in 1967 and 1968, *The Prisoner* is one of most discussed television dramas of all time. McGoohan's 'Number 6' character refuses to cooperate with the inhabitants of The Village, despite various underhand methods used to break his will. He finally escapes in a controversial and confusing final episode that leaves many of the questions raised by the show unanswered. The enigmatic series has spawned societies and fan clubs whose members still pore over scripts like Biblical scholars in an effort to understand *The Prisoner*'s hidden meanings.

Patrick McGoohan was a big star at the time. He appeared in the popular spy drama *Danger Man*, giving performances that impressed the James Bond team enough to offer him the role of 007. But he turned it down and, together with George Markstein, created *The Prisoner*. It was an iconic and instantly recognizable show: the unusual location of Portmeirion in Wales (a town whose Italianate architecture made it look more Mediterranean than Welsh), Ron Grainer's memorable music, the frequent psychedelic visual effects and the show's Orwellian themes all contributed to make *The Prisoner* compulsive viewing.

The Prisoner's large cult following presumably includes one or two of the writers of *The Simpsons*. There have been several allusions to *The Prisoner* in this show, including an episode where Marge tries to escape from a religious cult only to be pursued and caught by a large white balloon. In *The Prisoner*, a similar balloon, known as 'Rover', was used to capture Number 2 whenever he tried to escape from The Village.

I could do that

⇨ See **Gizza job**

I didn't expect the Spanish Inquisition

⇨ See **Monty Python's Flying Circus**

I didn't get where I am today ...

The Fall and Rise of Reginald Perrin

Reggie Perrin, now successful owner of a chain of shops selling expensive rubbish, meets his old boss CJ and inquires about the downward fortunes of the company that once employed him. The response is couched in predictable terms: 'We've entered a slight wobble. I didn't get where I am today without knowing a slight wobble when I enter one.'

'I didn't get where I am today ...' is the catchphrase of CJ, the boss of pudding manufacturers Sunshine Desserts in the British sitcom *The Fall and Rise of Reginald Perrin*, written by David Nobbs. Over four series, starting in 1976, it told the tale of its eponymous hero's mid-life crisis, faked suicide, and eventual business success running an empire of shops offering useless gifts. Leonard Rossiter starred in the title role of a show that also featured one of television's most memorable bad bosses. Played by John Barron, CJ terrified his underlings but was never reticent about singing his own praises with reflections that always started with the words 'I didn't get where I am today ...'

Other characters had catchphrases too: Reggie's brother-in-law Jimmy (Geoffrey Palmer) always needed to borrow food from the Perrins, explaining that there had been a 'bit of a cock-up on the catering front'; meanwhile, CJ's two yes-men, Tony Webster (Trevor Adams) and David Harris-Jones (Bruce Bold), expressed their loyalty by responding to everything he said with 'Great!' and 'Super!' respectively.

CJ's catchphrase lives on in, of all places, a vegetarian restaurant in Plymouth. Called Veggie Perrin's, this meat-free eatery advertises itself with the words, 'I didn't get where I am today by eating meat! There's no cock-up on the catering front at Veggie Perrins!'

72

I don't believe it!

One Foot in the Grave

What had Victor Meldrew ever done to deserve such continual calamity and humiliation? This was the question viewers of *One Foot in the Grave* posed as they watched the hapless pensioner become entangled in a long series of messes that left the unfortunate senior citizen exclaiming '**I don't believe it!**'

One Foot in the Grave, written by David Renwick and running from 1990 to 2000, became one of the BBC's best-loved sitcoms, despite initially being greeted with indifference by the critics. Concerning the lives of a newly retired suburban couple, Victor (Richard Wilson) and Margaret (Annette Crosbie), it pitted the ironically named Victor against all the most frustrating aspects of modern life. These were made even worse by bad luck, coincidences and misunderstandings, which always left Victor up to his neck (sometimes literally) in bizarre and humiliating situations, usually witnessed by his neighbours.

Victor does not set out to be a pessimist or curmudgeon – in one episode he is seen laughing uproariously while listening to a *Monty Python* record on his headphones – but the bad luck that plagues him can't help but bring out these qualities. His rants against inefficient and indifferent workmen, garage mechanics, call centres and bureaucrats seemed to sum up a particular type of person. So much so that anyone who makes a grumpy remark now runs the risk of being called a **Victor Meldrew**.

One Foot in the Grave ended on a characteristically dark note in November 2000. On a wet night, Victor was run over by a car, ending ten years of black comedy and saddening millions of viewers. Some fans even left flowers by the scene of the accident, a tribute to the skill of both writer and actor who combined to make Victor Meldrew one of comedy's most memorable characters.

His catchphrase 'I don't believe it!' caught on very quickly. Although the producer of the show tried to restrict its use in order to maintain the phrase's impact, it soon became identified with the character. Actor Richard Wilson was plagued by people repeating the catchphrase, a fact that was memorably satirized in an episode of *Father Ted* where Wilson (playing himself) ends up attacking Ted after the priest does a particularly loud and mannered rendition of Victor's trademark words while the actor attempts to have a quiet day off at a tourist attraction.

… if it hadn't been for those pesky kids
Scooby-Doo

The criminals in *Scooby-Doo* were always enraged that they had been outwitted by a group of teenagers and a talking dog. This feeling was expressed at the end of every episode when, about to be led away by police, the felon would exclaim, 'And I would have gotten away with it too, **if it hadn't been for those pesky kids**.'

Scooby-Doo is an animated Hanna-Barbera cartoon featuring the adventures of Fred, Shaggy, Velma and Daphne, who drive about in a psychedelically painted van and call themselves 'Mystery, Inc.' They are assisted by their Great Dane, after whom the show is named. Although Scooby and Shaggy are cowardly and Daphne is frequently rendered useless by the loss of her glasses, the gang always manage to solve whatever mystery they happen to be embroiled in. At the outset, whatever strange goings-on are encountered appear to have supernatural causes, but the teenagers end up finding a rational explanation. This always involves a criminal trying to cover his villainous tracks by pretending to be a ghost or an alien. The crook is led into a trap, with Shaggy and Scooby used as bait, then caught and handed over to the authorities. After the criminal's parting words, Scooby is rewarded with a **Scooby snack**, usually a giant multi-layered sandwich which the crime-fighting hound consumes in one gulp.

Although formulaic, the cartoon has been very popular since its first broadcast in 1969. It has been referred to or pastiched in a number of other films and TV series, most notably *Wayne's World* and *Buffy the Vampire Slayer*. In *Buffy*, the monster-slaying heroine and her companions refer to themselves as the Scooby Gang, although, mercifully, a binge-eating talking canine is not part of her crew.

I have a cunning plan

The Black Adder

'**I have a cunning plan**' is a phrase especially associated with Baldrick, the dim-witted servant played by Tony Robinson opposite Rowan Atkinson's Edmund in *The Black Adder* and its sequels. Baldrick's schemes to extricate his master from dangerous situations are never well thought out and always result in a withering remark from the sneering Edmund. Edmund is not averse to a cunning plan himself, although the outcome of these is – at best – mixed.

One of Britain's favourite situation comedies, the *Blackadder* sequence tells the tale of four disparate generations of selfish but somehow admirable schemers called Edmund Blackadder. In *The Black Adder* the action is set in the Middle Ages and Edmund is a prince. Over time the Blackadder line becomes increasingly less noble: in *Blackadder II*, set in the court of Elizabeth I, Edmund is a peer; in *Blackadder the Third* he is butler to the Prince Regent; and finally, in *Blackadder Goes Forth*, our hero has no royal connections, being a career officer in the British Army during World War I.

The first series, written by Rowan Atkinson and Richard Curtis 'with additional dialogue by William Shakespeare', was shown in 1983, and was very expensive, involving a large cast and many outdoor locations. As a result the show was almost cancelled by the BBC, but it was saved when the budget for the second series was scaled down and filming restricted to the studio. Changes to the scripting and characters also took place: Ben Elton took over writing duties from Rowan Atkinson, and Edmund's character became much more intelligent. Baldrick's IQ went in the other direction and the intellectual mismatch stayed fairly constant for the remaining series.

Besides Robinson and Atkinson, other cast regulars included Stephen Fry (the Duke of Wellington and two members of the aristocratic Melchett family), Hugh Laurie (Prince George and Lieutenant George), Miranda Richardson (Queen Elizabeth I) and Tim McInnerny (Lord Percy and Captain Darling). Tom Baker, Robbie Coltrane and Rik Mayall contributed memorable cameo roles.

The fourth series ended in 1989, but the *Blackadder* franchise has remained hugely popular. Baldrick has not been forgotten, and his famous catchphrase is often alluded to. In 2002, for example, *The Times*, reporting on the reorganization of Britain's railways, talked about 'a cunning plan which, ultimately, will shunt Railtrack into the forgotten sidings of history'.

I'll get me coat

The Fast Show

Many of us have at one time or another experienced the feeling of being out of our depth in a particular type of company. In extreme cases, it appears that the best course of action is simply to leave without further ado, and this situation can be alluded to with the expression '**I'll get me coat**.'

This is the catchphrase of an anonymous character played by Mark Williams in *The Fast Show* (see page 183), who regularly and inexplicably finds himself part of a middle-class group with highbrow tastes and an urbane line in conversation. With no pretensions to intellect and more down-to-earth proclivities, Williams's character inevitably pitches in with a comment that results in withering looks and embarrassed silence. Realizing the seriousness of his gaffe, he does not even pretend to make any excuses for his hasty departure. 'I'll get me coat' suffices.

> "You know mini-kievs, yeah? On the menu would they be under starters or main courses? . . . I'll get me coat."

Effective in its very simplicity, the phrase has come to sum up the embarrassment of finding oneself surrounded by beautiful people, intellectual heavyweights or just poseurs, especially when one has just given oneself away by making an inappropriate remark.

I love it when a plan comes together
The A-Team

For schoolboys in the 1980s there was only one way to savour success or victory: not with a wild celebration but rather a contented smile, a puff on an imaginary cigar and the line '**I love it when a plan comes together**'.

The catchphrase was employed on a regular basis by George Peppard in his role as Colonel John 'Hannibal' Smith in *The A-Team*, a tongue-in-cheek American drama series that featured four Vietnam veterans wrongly accused of 'a crime they didn't commit'. While on the run from the authorities, the A-Team still found time to fight for the persecuted and dispossessed. Hannibal was the suave leader of the quartet, which also comprised hard-man mechanic BA Baracus (played by Mr T), 'Howling Mad' Murdock, the team's pilot and resident lunatic (Dwight Schultz), and silver-tongued ladies' man Templeton 'Faceman' Peck (Dirk Benedict).

For five seasons and 98 episodes from 1983 to 1987 the A-Team fought the bad guys, invariably using a mixture of ludicrous disguises, hastily erected weaponry and a good line in wry humour to win through. Remarkably, given the amount of gun-toting in the show, only one character was ever actually shot and killed.

In fact, the role of Hannibal Smith was hardly the culmination of a glorious plan for Peppard. In 1961, as a promising young actor, he had starred alongside Audrey Hepburn in *Breakfast at Tiffany's*. However, his roles declined over the years and he battled with alcoholism, until the opportunity came to play Hannibal, the role which was to define his career. Peppard died in 1994, robbing fans of the chance to see him reprise the character in the much-anticipated film version of the series.

I'm free

Are You Being Served?

It may seem hard to believe in these days when shops often seem to be staffed exclusively by charmless youths whose sole purpose is to get customers to sign up for extortionate store cards and unnecessarily extended warranties, but there was a time when shopping in Britain was a much more genteel experience. Floorwalkers would greet customers at the door and politely ask sir or madam what they wished to purchase. This fast-fading retail world was portrayed in *Are You Being Served?* where senior salesman Captain Peacock (Frank Thornton) would ask his juniors if they were available to serve a customer, prompting the response '**I'm free.**'

Are You Being Served? was written by Jeremy Lloyd and David Croft and ran from 1972 to 1985 on BBC1. Set in the fictional Grace Brothers department store, its mix of class-based humour and sub-*Carry On* innuendo proved a hit with audiences first in the UK and later in the USA. Grace Brothers was staffed by a team of over-the-top characters, the most OTT of all being Mr Humphreys. Played by John Inman, Mr Humphreys was an extraordinarily camp sales assistant who had a mincing walk and lived with his mother. Instead of a decorous 'I'm free' to Captain Peacock's inquiries, Mr Humphreys would positively sing out his playfully affirmative response, much to the delight of the studio audience.

Readers of the *TV Times* voted Inman 'Funniest Man on TV' in 1976, and he cashed in on his popularity by releasing a number of records. His rendition of 'Teddy Bears' Picnic' was a favourite with junior audiences while 'I'm Free!' exploited the catchphrase of his alter ego.

'I'm free' is still one of British television's best loved catchphrases. In an era when you can download sounds to use on your mobile phone, John Inman's words are more than holding their own (ooh er!) with the likes of 'Booyakasha!' in the comedy ringtone charts.

I'm listening

Frasier

Callers to Dr Frasier Crane's show on the radio station KACL in Seattle sought advice in dealing with their personal problems. The host, with a rich and mellifluous voice oozing empathy and wisdom, put them at ease then asked them to relate their problems with the words '**I'm listening**.'

If the callers had known Dr Crane personally, they might not have sought his advice so readily. Throughout his screen life, the interfering, snobbish and egotistical psychiatrist failed to practise what he preached. He was the last man any of his callers should have adopted as a role model.

The character of Frasier Crane, played by Kelsey Grammer, first appeared in *Cheers*, a hugely popular situation comedy set in a Boston bar. Overeducated and uptight, Frasier was a fish out of water in the easy-going bar-room milieu, but he loosened up gradually and the regulars eventually warmed to him. When *Cheers* ended, Dr Crane moved to Seattle and became the main star of the most successful spin-off in television history, *Frasier*.

The comedy of *Frasier* stems from a number of sources: sibling rivalry between Frasier and his brother Niles (David Hyde Pierce), who is also a psychiatrist and shares many of his older brother's interests and neuroses; class tensions between the classically educated brothers and the blue-collar characters such as radio producer Roz Doyle (Peri Gilpin) and the Crane boys' father, Martin (John Mahoney), an ex-cop who has been invalided out of the force; and, finally, romance. Failed relationships litter the show. Both Crane brothers had disastrous first marriages and Frasier's dates always end in failure. Niles harbours a lengthy secret love for Daphne Moon (Jane Leeves), his father's English live-in health worker. But this unlikely relationship has a happy ending: after many years of keeping his feelings to himself, he finally expresses his yearning for the daffy Mancunian and the two end up getting married and having a baby.

From 1993 to 2004, *Frasier* provided television with some of its sharpest comedy. Large viewing figures and a staggering 37 Emmys amply rewarded a show which is universally considered a classic.

'm not fat, I'm big-boned

See **South Park**

Is it because I is black?

⇨ See **Booyakasha!**

Is that your final answer?

⇨ See **Who Wants to Be a Millionaire?**

It's life, Jim, but not as we know it

Star Trek

In most episodes of the original series of *Star Trek* (see page 174), grouchy Dr Leonard McCoy (played by DeForest Kelly) could usually be relied on to bluster 'I'm a doctor, not a mechanic', or 'engineer', or 'coal miner' or even (in the episode 'Return of the Archons') 'a flesh peddler', when asked to do anything beyond his job description.

When he wasn't being grumpy, 'Bones' (as he was affectionately known to his friend Captain James Kirk) would spend a lot of his time waving a tiny buzzing scanner thing over bodies and analysing the results. When the body belonged to a particularly strange life form, he would look up at Captain Kirk with furrowed brow and utter the words '**It's life, Jim, but not as we know it**.'

The phrase, often suitably modified, has been assimilated into the English language and is used when you want to convey that you're talking about a particularly unconventional example of something, often with the implication that you don't approve. The word 'life' can be replaced by almost anything: 'It's an Indian restaurant, Jim, but not as we know it', 'It's street theatre, Jim, but not as we know it', and so on. Other items to have been slotted into the formula include 'the law', 'an orchard', 'computing', 'Anglicanism', '4-4-2', 'comedy', 'the Internet', 'American football', 'golf', 'spirituality' and even 'television'. In fact, 'It's television, Jim, but not as we know it' could have made a suitable description of *Star Trek* itself when it was first broadcast.

A good test of whether a catchphrase has become a living part of the language is to see if writers can shorten it without their readers missing the allusion. Dr McCoy's catchphrase passed this test in November 2004 when a headline in the *Observer*'s review section read simply: 'It's theatre, Jim'.

I've started so I'll finish
Mastermind

Mastermind is perhaps the most nerve-wracking of all television quiz programmes, the intimidating atmosphere being set from the beginning by the aptly named theme tune 'Approaching Menace'. This is no accident: its creator Bill Wright took the idea from his experience of being interrogated while a prisoner of war in World War II. Just as prisoners would answer three questions (name, rank and number), so contestants have to state their name, occupation and specialist subject. The black leather chair (surely one of the most famous of TV artefacts), the spotlight and the unseen countdown all add to the tension.

Magnus Magnusson presented the show throughout its original run from 1972 to 1997, and is still inextricably linked with the programme. After a brief revival on the Discovery Channel with Clive Anderson as host, it was relaunched on the BBC in 2003 with John Humphrys now asking the questions. Celebrity specials and a junior edition have also followed.

None of those following in Magnus's footsteps have dared to dispense with his famous catchphrase, '**I've started so I'll finish**'. These words were uttered whenever the quizmaster was in mid-question when the buzzer went at the end of the allotted two minutes. Because it is hard to beat as a neat way of expressing that one is going to carry on with an activity regardless of any interruption or change of mind, the phrase has become part of the language and could be used of activities as diverse as stripping wallpaper, dieting or reading a dull book. It was hardly surprising, then, that Magnusson chose it as the title of his 1997 book about the history of the programme.

The show's other great contribution to our language was '**pass**', the word that contestants were required to say when they didn't know the answer and wanted to move on to the next question. This word is now routinely used in many TV quiz programmes as well as everyday conversation.

It is indicative of *Mastermind*'s status in British television that two legendary TV comedy shows have paid homage to it: the programme was parodied on more than one occasion by *The Morecambe and Wise Show*, while one of the most ingenious sketches from *The Two Ronnies* involves Ronnie Corbett as a contestant whose specialist subject is 'Answering the question before last'.

I want that one

Little Britain

The BBC's comedy show *Little Britain* is written by and stars comedians Matt Lucas and David Walliams (apparently there was already a David Williams), with a surreal voice-over gleefully provided by Tom Baker.

One of the sketches in this character-based series features caring and compassionate Lou (played by Walliams) and his unresponsive and manipulative friend Andy (played by Lucas). Lou spends his time looking after Andy, who is confined to a wheelchair and constantly makes arbitrary choices about his likes and dislikes. Lou struggles to satisfy these, only to have Andy casually change his mind when it is too late. Andy's catchphrase '**I want that one**' has been adapted by fans to numerous situations and invariably generates hilarity (at least in the short term).

The sketches featuring Lou and Andy follow a regular formula (although the scenarios have tended to get more extreme over time): Lou offers Andy a choice (the colour of his room, a holiday destination, a book from the library); Andy then makes an arbitrary decision, often not even looking, gesticulates vaguely and insists, 'I want that one'; Lou patiently questions Andy's irrational choice; Andy responds, 'Yeah, definitely want that one'; Lou gets Andy what he wants; finally, Andy responds, 'I don't like that one.'

Unbeknown to Lou, Andy is completely able-bodied, and lopes about doing things for himself while Lou's back is turned. In one sketch, Lou is talking to a swimming-pool attendant about facilities for his disabled friend, during which time Andy (seen in the background) hops out of his chair, climbs to the highest diving board, drops into the pool, swims to the side and climbs back into his chair just as Lou turns round.

Oddly for a show that makes so much of the visual possibilities offered by the medium of television, *Little Britain* was originally broadcast on BBC Radio 4 in 2002. The first TV series was broadcast on BBC3 in 2003, with another series following in 2004.

I was very, very drunk

The Fast Show

The disclaimer '**I was very, very drunk**' is a very handy one to add to tales of one's escapades while under the influence.

The phrase was made popular by Rowley Birkin QC, a permanently plastered ex-barrister played by Paul Whitehouse in *The Fast Show* (see page 183), who is said to have been based on a similar character Whitehouse once met while on holiday in Iceland. Birkin sits by the fire, whisky glass in hand, and recalls his salad days in an incoherent, impenetrable ramble interspersed with the occasional lucid and highly intriguing phrase ('... Her husband had been entombed in ice ...'). However, inebriation is clearly not a new experience for the old boy, with every story ending in the admission 'I was very, very drunk.'

With a 'drinking culture' alive and well in Britain, this catchphrase was bound to become a favourite from the show if any was, and it can still be heard whenever and wherever people are recounting things they did after one too many drinks had been consumed – in other words, quite often.

I weel zay zis only once ...

'Allo, 'Allo!

'Allo, 'Allo! was an internationally successful situation comedy that ran on the BBC over nine series and 85 episodes between 1985 and 1992. Gorden Kaye played René Artois, a bumbling café owner who becomes unwittingly involved with the French Resistance as plans are made to smuggle two British airmen back home. René's life is complicated: he is married to the formidable Edith (Carmen Silvera) and trying to maintain an affair with sexy waitress Yvette Carte-Blanche (Vicki Michelle). Not surprisingly, this adds an element of farce to the proceedings. Life is further complicated by frequent visits to René's establishment by the German Army and the SS.

Comic goings-on in Nazi-occupied France may at first sight seem a dubious subject for humour, but the show made fun not so much of the war but of film and TV dramas that dealt with the war, in particular the BBC drama about the Resistance movement, *Secret Army*, starring Bernard Hepton, which ran from 1977 to 1982. Its penchant for farce and bawdy humour positioned *'Allo, 'Allo!* well away from reality and any possibility of causing offence, and it was a huge hit on French TV.

The show had a novel method of dealing with the bilingual milieu in which the characters operated. French characters spoke in English with exaggerated French accents to show they were speaking French, and when they attempted English they adopted equally exaggerated posh Oxford accents. English characters spoke English normally, but spoke French with a bad, almost incomprehensible 'English' French accent, a favourite being 'good moaning' instead of 'good morning'. The phrase '**I weel zay zis only once**' was originally used by Resistance leader Michelle Dubois (Kirsten Cooke) as a prelude to relaying vital information and has subsequently been adopted as a catchphrase when communicating anything important.

Incidentally, the odd spelling of Gorden Kaye's first name was apparently due to an Equity typing error, but the actor himself maintained that it was 'the sign of a misspelt youth'.

Izzy wizzy, let's get busy
The Sooty Show

Believe it or not, Sooty celebrated his fiftieth birthday in 1998. But despite being listed in *The Guinness Book of Records* as the star of the longest running children's television show, the diminutive prestidigitator and lovable scamp had nothing to say for himself.

Sooty's catchphrase '**Izzy wizzy, let's get busy**' was used prior to launching into some ill-fated conjuring routine. For a long while it was uttered on his behalf by Matthew Corbett, who worked for many years as Sooty's 'right hand man'. People who grew up watching the bear's disastrous attempts to do tricks with flour and buckets of water have sometimes been heard to repeat the phrase when exhorting colleagues to set about a new task.

Sooty's meteoric rise to fame began when a yellow bear-shaped glove-puppet was spotted by Matthew Corbett's father Harry in a joke shop on Blackpool Pier in 1948. Harry Corbett, an amateur magician, introduced 'Teddy' into his act and won a TV spot via a talent show. He and his little pal were signed to the BBC on the condition that the bear was altered, so Harry blackened the golden bear's ears with chimney soot and, hey presto, 'Teddy' was miraculously transformed into 'Sooty'.

After 25 years of success during which co-stars Sweep and Soo joined the act, Sooty was handed from father to son after Harry Corbett suffered a heart attack in 1975. Another 25 years on, Sooty changed hands again, with Matthew Corbett retiring and co-presenters Richard Cadell and Liana Bridges taking over. Corbett's parting comment was, 'It's time Sooty stood on his own two feet.'

jumpers for goalposts

The Fast Show

The expression '**jumpers for goalposts**' expresses a hankering for the days when association football was played by gentlemen and the Corinthian spirit ruled, an era when promising young players were not pampered in football academies, but honed their skills in the street and in the local park, playing for the pure love of the game.

The phrase was popularized by the character of Ron Manager in *The Fast Show* (see page 183), an ex-manager-turned-pundit whose dewy-eyed nostalgia usually carried him away into complete nonsense. It has been suggested that Paul Whitehouse, who played this character, based him on the late Alec Stock, an old-school gent who managed Orient, Queens Park Rangers and Fulham in the 1950s, 1960s and 1970s and was the sort of manager whose team talks were peppered with quotations from Browning and Kipling.

> "It's a far cry from small boys in the park, jumpers for goalposts. Isn't it? Mmmmm. Marvellous!"

In a time of cynical professionalism, when harassed managers are more inclined to attempt to motivate their overpaid charges with tirades of profanity, the catchphrase 'jumpers for goalposts' has come to stand for a generation that looks back wistfully to a time when everything – not only football – was much, much better.

just like that

The Tommy Cooper Hour

Tommy Cooper was a unique comic performer, adored by his millions of fans but also acclaimed by his peers as one of the best in the business. Like Eric Morecambe, his mere presence on stage would get the audience smiling. Indeed, viewers would be laughing out loud long before Cooper even performed his first trick or uttered his catchphrase '**just like that**'.

Tommy Cooper was a magician who made a career out of getting magic tricks wrong. He started performing as a soldier in Egypt, where he was stationed during World War II. Missing a helmet required as a prop for his act one day, he quickly grabbed a waiter's fez and the laughs it generated made it a part of Cooper's act until the day he died.

Cooper's first TV appearances, in the late 1940s, were as a supporting act in variety shows, but he quickly rose up the bill, and eventually starred in his own shows such as *The Tommy Cooper Hour* (1957), *Cooperama* (1966) and *Cooper – Just Like That* (1978).

The phrase 'just like that' was ostensibly used as a commentary on the piece of sleight of hand he was demonstrating. However, as the tricks never worked out first time, it often had to be followed by 'not like that', as he covered up for his apparent mistakes. He said his catchphrase for the last time in 1984, the year in which he died after suffering a heart attack on stage during a recording of the show *Live from Her Majesty's*. The audience assumed that Cooper's collapse was a designed part of his comedy routine and continued to laugh and cheer for some time.

just one more thing
Columbo

The American detective drama *Columbo* is probably better known for its visual props than its linguistic innovation. His rumpled raincoat, his cigar, his beat-up old car and his sad-eyed pet basset hound all made the character of Lieutenant Frank Columbo, played by Peter Falk, immediately recognizable. Indeed the show made much play of the dishevelled (anyone writing about the character of Columbo is contractually obliged to use this word) appearance of the Los Angeles detective: when he appeared at the crime scene, he often seemed to be on the verge of being arrested for vagrancy before revealing that he was in fact the detective assigned to the case.

Once on the case, however, Columbo could be relied on to nail the murderer. Indeed the shambolic appearance proved to be part of his technique to put the killer off guard. (The performance of the murder was shown at the start of each episode, thus focussing the attention on the process of detection rather than guessing the identity of the murderer.) Columbo's initial questioning of the murderer would always be apparently harmless but, just at the point of leaving, the detective would turn around and say casually, '**just one more thing**'. This formula invariably began the process of tripping up the killer by exposing the inconsistencies in the elaborate murder plan, and from then on it was only a matter of time before the jig was up.

Columbo was first broadcast in 1968 and remained a regular feature of the American schedules until 1977. The programme's immense popularity has led to it being revived several times subsequently. Like the detective himself, it seems that just when you think it has disappeared it keeps coming back for just one more.

Just say no

Grange Hill

The comprehensive-school drama series *Grange Hill* has been a mainstay of the BBC's children's broadcasting since 1978. It is slightly curious, however, that the phrase with which it is most associated, '**Just say no**', should have been popularized through a cast record rather than by the programme itself.

Grange Hill has seldom been shy about tackling difficult issues, and in 1986 it ran a ground-breaking storyline in which the popular character Zammo Maguire (played by Lee MacDonald) fell prey to heroin addiction – strong stuff indeed for children's tea-time viewing. The producers of the show tied the storyline in with the slogan 'Just say no', which was being strongly promoted at the time by America's First Lady Nancy Reagan as part of an anti-drugs campaign being waged in schools in the USA. The cast of *Grange Hill* followed Mrs Reagan's cue and released a single called 'Just Say No' which reached a creditable number 5 in the UK charts.

The record may not have achieved its goal of removing the menace of drugs from British society, but the phrase 'Just say no' has become firmly rooted in the language. Not only is it trotted out frequently as a plea to young people to refuse offers of drugs, but it has also been applied to other issues: atheists urge us 'Just say no to God'; Friends of the Earth have called on us to 'just say no' to genetically modified crops; and in 2001 arch-Eurosceptic politician John Redwood even published a book entitled *Just Say No: 100 Arguments Against the Euro*.

Keep 'em peeled

Police Five

This injunction to stay alert and watchful first appeared in the form 'Keep your eye peeled!' in a Missouri newspaper of 1853 and, by the late 19th century, variations on the expression 'Keep your eyes peeled' were to be found in print on both sides of the Atlantic. The later, chattier variant **'Keep 'em peeled'** was the trademark parting advice of Shaw Taylor, the well-coiffed and besuited presenter of ITV's *Police Five.*

This series ran for almost thirty years, starting in 1962 and finally going off duty in 1990. Each episode outlined the circumstances of a handful of as-yet-unsolved crimes in the London area – regional equivalents were screened in other areas – with the aim of eliciting viewers' help in tracking down the criminals responsible. Reporting from the scene, Taylor would employ his blend of scoutmasterly concern and avuncular charm to jog the memory or prick the conscience of potential witnesses, with the question 'Were you in the neighbourhood?' regularly delivered to camera.

Produced in conjunction with Scotland Yard, the series was a forerunner of the BBC's more high-tech *Crimewatch UK* and also spawned a children's version, *Junior Police Five*, in the 1970s. The creation of the first Neighbourhood Watch scheme in 1982 must owe something to the climate of neighbourly watchfulness that *Police Five* helped to create, and now over 6 million UK households are 'keeping 'em peeled' on a regular basis.

Klingon

⇨ See **Star Trek**

Kojak

Kojak

In the 1970s, if you wanted to allude to the fact that a man was bald, you might refer to him as **'Kojak'**. Replacing 'baldy', this term remained a popular insult until 'slaphead' and 'chrome dome' stole its crown.

The name refers to Theo Kojak, a hard-bitten New York cop, who was the eponymous hero of a police drama that ran from 1973 to 1978. Played by Telly Savalas, the Greek-American detective's no-nonsense style and disdain for his bosses made him popular with audiences around the world. He was also, by virtue of his bald head and penchant for lollipops (which he sucked as a substitute for the cigarettes he was trying to give up), an easy target for impressionists, who would also pick up on his catchphrase **'Who loves ya, baby?'**

Savalas cashed in on the popularity of the show, releasing a record called – yes, you've guessed it – 'Who Loves Ya, Baby?' This rather predictably named recording was followed by a more surprising musical project: a spoken version of the David Gates song 'If'. This single, despite its dubious merits, topped the charts for two weeks in 1975.

Kojak is still regarded as an epitome of baldness, but another of the character's associations has proved more ephemeral: although he worked in a very busy city, the need to keep the action moving meant that the show's hero rarely had difficulty in finding a parking space. This point did not go unnoticed, and for a time the verb 'to kojak' entered American slang with the meaning 'to find a parking space in an area where such discoveries are at best rare'.

Let's be careful out there
Hill Street Blues

Hill Street Blues was the ongoing story of an overworked police precinct in inner-city America. It followed the lives of numerous often heroic but flawed characters at every level of the force.

Most episodes began with the morning roll-call, and this produced the show's best-known and most imitated phrase. Fatherly Sergeant Phil Esterhaus (Michael Conrad) made announcements and assigned duties in an atmosphere of comradeship and calm before the day's storm. Esterhaus ended each roll-call with the same words: 'And, hey – **let's be careful out there**.' The character was killed off in 1983, after Michael Conrad's death, to be replaced by Sergeant Stan Jablonski (Robert Prosky), whose catchphrase was a bit more proactive: 'Let's do it to them before they do it to us.'

It was Conrad's sentiment that struck a chord, however, and it often came to be used ironically. The cops of the Hill Street Precinct were sent out to keep the peace among gun-toting crackheads, but these days you are quite likely to use the phrase 'Let's be careful out there' to people who are going to encounter nothing more menacing than a truculent photocopier as they go about their business.

NBC screened 146 episodes of *Hill Street Blues* between 1981 and 1987. The programme was praised for its combination of drama and comedy and fine ensemble acting, and was shot in a then-radical documentary style, with continuous storylines running across episodes, and long and hand-held camera shots being used. This format paved the way for a new, more gritty style of TV, exemplified by programmes such as *St Elsewhere*, *NYPD Blue* and *ER*.

The show's realism did not extend to setting *Hill Street Blues* in a particular city, however. The action was supposed to take place somewhere on the east coast, but the opening credit sequence was shot in Chicago, and the episodes themselves were mostly shot in Los Angeles, where the producers waged a constant struggle to find locations that were sufficiently free of palm trees.

Let's have a look at the old scoreboard
⇨ See **The Generation Game**

ike

Friends

It is probably only human nature to complain that things are not what they used to be. In 2003 the programme *Grumpy Old Men* cashed in on this tendency, lining up middle-aged celebrities to rant about the follies of the younger generation.

Alongside predictable swipes at tastes in music and fashion, there was much lamentation about the declining standard of spoken English, with the American sitcom *Friends* (see page 54) being cited as an especially malign influence on the speech of the young, and the use of the word **'like'** on that show being singled out for particular censure.

Language purists grew up in the certainty that there are two ways of reporting what a person said: you can use direct speech, which involves a verb of speaking ('I said'; 'she cried'; 'he uttered') followed by a set of inverted commas containing the speaker's exact words; or you can use indirect speech, which generally involves the word 'that' followed by a paraphrase of what was actually said ('I said that I was sorry').

But the way the characters in *Friends* speak often seems to blur these two methods. The typical introduction substitutes the phrase 'was like' for a verb of speaking ('I was like ...'; 'she was like ...'), and there follows what purports to be the speaker's exact words, apparently using the technique of direct speech.

But in fact the formula 'I was like ...' promises only an approximation of what the speaker actually said and may not even guarantee that anything was said at all. So when Phoebe says, 'For a minute there I was like, "Ooh, where'd Ross go?"', she is giving an indication of her thoughts rather than recording her exact words. No doubt it is the inexact nature of the formula that drives the traditionalists to distraction, while young people find it liberating for exactly the same reason.

In fact, Glaswegians were using a similar pattern of speech long before the advent of *Friends*, saying 'I was like that' accompanied by a gesture or facial expression that sums up the speaker's state of mind in a way that words are incapable of doing. But this fact is unlikely to stop many purists from railing against the modern use of 'like' as a sure sign of the end of civilization.

Loadsamoney

Friday Night Live

Comedian Harry Enfield first came to public notice on Channel 4's *Saturday Live* in 1985 (see page 145). But it was on this show's successor *Friday Night Live* in 1988 that he introduced a comic character who not only made the nation laugh but also summed up the mood of the times in one word: **Loadsamoney**. This creation was a loud, vulgar plasterer who shamelessly flaunted the wads of cash he earned. This was a time when many in the south of England were enjoying the profits of a property boom, and Enfield and his writing partner Paul Whitehouse identified, better and more quickly than any sociologist, a new type of individual who was emerging as a result: the Thatcher-supporting working-class self-made man.

Left-wing politicians and journalists eagerly seized upon the new word and used the idea of a 'Loadsamoney society' as a means of attacking their Thatcherite opponents. Regrettably for the Left, however, the people whom Enfield satirized were quite unashamed to be associated with Loadsamoney and viewed the materialistic builder as a hero. For this reason, Enfield killed off the character at the height of his popularity (although not before he cashed in with a spin-off hit single).

Enfield recognized that Loadsamoneys were restricted mainly to south-east England and that the fruits of the Thatcher revolution were not being enjoyed in many other parts of Britain. This north–south divide was expressed comedically in Enfield's next creation for *Friday Night Live*: Buggerallmoney, an unemployed chain-smoking Geordie with a Chris-Waddle-style mullet haircut. A counterpoint to Loadsamoney, his lack of financial success was expressed in the defiant but defensive motto, 'I've got bugger-all money but I'm that hard!'

'Loadsamoney' was the right word at the right time and quickly became established in British English, finding its way into many dictionaries – both as a noun and an adjective – just a few years after the character was created.

lovely jubbly
⇨ See **Only Fools and Horses**

94

END OF
PART ONE

and now some
words from our
sponsors

and all because the lady loves ...

Cadbury's Milk Tray

A dashingly handsome hero, known only as the Man in Black, goes to extraordinary lengths – diving off high cliffs, battling man-eating sharks, skiing down fearsomely steep mountains – to deposit a box of chocolates on the dressing-table of his mysterious lady friend. Not only does he go through hell and high water to deliver the delicious confectionery, but he makes a quick exit without helping himself to the coffee creams. The voice-over then tells us that the preceding adventure was '**all because the lady loves Milk Tray**'.

Every woman's dream? Well, it certainly seemed to be between 1968 and 2000 when Cadbury's used a series of mini-epics featuring a hero in the James Bond mould to advertise their most popular box of chocolates. Then, in 2002, the ad-men declared the Man in Black too macho and gave him the boot. He collected his P45, hung up his trademark black polo-neck sweater and bid viewers farewell as the new slogans 'love with a lighter touch' and 'now with extra mmm and ahh' were rolled out.

The phrase still endures, though. Most years at least one newspaper or magazine will print a feature of gift ideas for Valentine's Day headed 'And all because the lady loves ...' Perhaps the Man in Black was pensioned off too soon.

anytime, anyplace, anywhere
Martini

A recent list of the 100 greatest ever TV adverts included at number 35 the 1970 Martini advert, with its slogan, '**Anytime, anyplace, anywhere**, / There's a wonderful world you can share.' If you don't regard at least the first line of this couplet as a classic, you are most definitely in the minority. Not only does everyone seem to know the line, but it has also been used in a variety of other areas, becoming part of contemporary culture to a remarkable degree.

This phrase has been self-consciously exploited in marketing material for, amongst other things, travel insurance, interactive computer software, the Royal Marines, the National Health Service, the Canine Film Academy, the Blackpool Hilton, goldfish ('the Martini of the pond world') and the Martini escort agency.

Advertising has certainly paid off for the firm of Martini and Rossi, whose brand of vermouth has become so famous that it has even eclipsed the generic name. (You would probably get a funny look if you went into a bar and asked for a dry vermouth rather than a dry Martini.) But there is a distinction between the brand name (spelt with a capital letter) and a martini (without a capital letter), which is a combination of gin or vodka and any vermouth you like, generally nowadays in the ratio 1:8 (earlier drinkers preferred 1:4), with the addition of ice and a green olive. Lovers of the martini have included Frank Sinatra, Sean Connery, Hunter S Thompson, Ernest Hemingway, Dorothy Parker, Lauren Bacall, Dean Martin, Ian Fleming, Tennessee Williams and W C Fields.

One issue that has never been resolved is what difference there might be between 'anyplace' and 'anywhere' as locations in which to enjoy 'the great taste of Martini'. Maybe the copywriter had enjoyed a few martinis (or Martinis) and simply thought it sounded good – which of course it does, so long as you don't think about it too hard.

because I'm worth it

L'Oréal

Although this has been the advertising slogan of L'Oréal haircare and cosmetic products since 1967, it is the celebrity-packed advertising campaigns of recent years – with actresses Andie MacDowell and Jennifer Aniston to the fore – that have resulted in the phrase '**because I'm worth it**' taking on a life of its own. Indeed, in the United States it has become something of a mantra for those with a high opinion of themselves. It is perhaps because the phrase has passed beyond the control of the advertisers that they decided to change it recently to the less egotistical 'because you're worth it'.

The narcissism of the original slogan is in contrast to the public-spirited catchphrase dreamed up by L'Oréal's founder, Eugène Schueller. In the 1930s he became involved in a national campaign to improve the health of France's children through cleanliness. This was done through repeated radio plays of Schueller's jaunty jingle '*Soyez propres, sentez bon!*' which translates as 'Be nice and clean, smell good!'

Just try getting Jennifer Aniston to sing that.

bootiful
Bernard Matthews' Turkey Drummers

Like Victor Kiam and Richard Branson, Bernard Matthews is a businessmen who believes in advertising his own wares. For many years he has been at the forefront of campaigns extolling the virtues of his Norfolk-farmed turkeys. The adverts, whether featuring joyful workers on the Matthews estate or cub scouts pining for Bernard Matthews' Turkey Drummers, all feature Bernard, a symphony in tweed, proclaiming his products to be really '**bootiful**'.

Bernard's characteristic pronunciation of the word 'beautiful' has long been synonymous with his products. Indeed, such is the power of advertising that, for people in the rest of the country, 'bootiful' has come to be virtually synonymous with Norfolk itself. Thus in 2001 *The Sun* could knowingly attach the word to a piece about a campaign to preserve the Norfolk dialect: 'National Lottery cash is helping keep alive the 'bootiful' Norfolk dialect made famous by turkey tycoon Bernard Matthews and 1960s star The Singing Postman.'

The same association was exploited by Norfolk boat designer Simon Sanderson. When he decided to make an assault on the world sailing speed record he chose the name *Bootiful* for his state-of-the-art catamaran. It is presumably no coincidence that his venture was being bankrolled by a certain local businessman called Bernard Matthews.

does exactly what it says on the tin
Ronseal Woodstain

Commercials for exciting products such as cars or beers often produce slogans that capture the imagination, but you might suspect wood dye is far too dull to lend itself to memorable advertising. So the makers of Ronseal Woodstain must have been delighted when their product became associated with a popular catchphrase.

The success story began in a Ronseal advertisement of the late 1980s in which a chirpy Everyman character explained that all the claims on the side of a container of Ronseal were true as Ronseal '**does exactly what it says on the tin**'. Over the following decade, this phrase, which roughly means 'What you see is what you get', gradually entered into everyday British speech until we have reached a point where everything from films to footballers and from works of art to wine can be described with this handy idiom.

A couple of examples show how far the phrase has come from its origins in the realm of household maintenance. In 1999, a cinema reviewer in *The Times* opined, 'The softened ending feels like a Hollywood compromise, alas, but otherwise *Cruel Intentions* does exactly what it says on the tin.' The same newspaper used the expression in 2001 when discussing a Turner Prize exhibit at the Tate Gallery: 'The piece Creed is displaying for the Turner exhibition is *Work 227: the lights going on and off.* Like all of his pieces, it does exactly what it says on the tin. In an empty gallery the lights go off every five seconds.'

Don't leave home without it!

American Express

We have become so accustomed to flashing the plastic when we shop that it is sometimes easy to forget that there was a time when buying goods with a plastic card was the exception rather than the rule. In the 1970s the American Express company had to make a determined effort to promote its card as a practical alternative to cash. It succeeded thanks to a slogan that has become an established reference point in popular culture.

In a long-running US advertising campaign created by Ogilvy & Mather, actor Karl Malden adopted his TV persona of Detective Mike Stone, star of *The Streets of San Francisco*, to promote the card. Malden's character appeared in a number of scenarios observing the problems that could befall the traveller who relied solely on cash, and noted the benefits that could accrue from ownership of the AmEx card, winding up with the message, 'American Express – **don't leave home without it!**'

Malden's crumpled Everyman persona enabled him to be accepted as a trusted source of financial advice, and this helped establish American Express as a prestigious provider of charge cards and traveller's cheques.

But the adverts have also left a rather more sinister legacy. Some people who live in places where crime is endemic feel that a revolver is of more use to them than a credit card when they venture out of doors. In such cases, they may jokingly refer to the gun as an 'AmEx'. If you ask them to explain the reason for the name, you are likely to get the answer, 'Because I don't leave home without it!'

⇨ See also **That'll do nicely, sir**

Everyone's a fruit and nut case

Cadbury's Fruit and Nut

The words '**Everyone's a fruit and nut case**, crazy for those Cadbury's nuts and raisins', were used in an advertisement for Cadbury's Fruit and Nut chocolate bar which first aired in 1977. The words were rendered more memorable by being set to 'The Dance of the Reed Flutes' from Tchaikovsky's ballet *The Nutcracker Suite*, an extremely catchy, floaty little tune, which is even now available as a ringtone for your mobile phone.

The word 'nutcase' had been used for a long time to refer to an insane person, and the advertisers were probably also influenced by the related idiom 'as nutty as a fruit cake'. The idea of combining a popular term for craziness with an intemperate desire for chocolate proved spectacularly successful, and 'fruit and nut case' has now to some extent replaced the older 'nutcase' as a term for anyone regarded as being dangerously unconventional.

The description 'fruit and nut case' even became a job title for DJ Sid Wilson of Slipknot, an American band that plays impossibly loud, aggressive music and performs extremely unpleasant stunts on stage.

Another self-confessed 'full-blown fruit and nut case' is Michael Newdow, the American atheist who filed a suit to prevent the Pledge of Allegiance from being recited in his daughter's classroom. Mr Newdow subsequently took up a public campaign to rid the English language of masculine and feminine pronouns, bidding to replace 'he' and 'she' with the gender-neutral 're'; 'his' and 'hers' with 'rees'; and 'him' and 'her' with 'erm'.

exceedingly good cakes

Mr Kipling

Before the 1960s most housewives bought cakes and pies from the local baker, but that all changed when big supermarkets and food manufacturers got in on the act, offering conveniently packaged tea-time treats on an industrial scale. The cake manufacturer Mr Kipling (founded in 1967, and part of the giant RHM food group) was at the forefront of this revolution. The brand adopted the name of one of Britain's best-loved writers to give it an air of Edwardian cosiness and gentility. This image was put forward for many years on television through adverts which featured the exploits of Mr Kipling as related by his friend. In each advert the friend would describe in mellifluous tones a scene from Mr Kipling's idyllic life – fishing, playing with a train set with his grandson, attending a village cricket match, etc – which always ended with the quintessential English gentleman providing his companions with a much-appreciated Battenberg cake or French Fancy as the friend remarked, 'Mr Kipling does make **exceedingly good cakes**.'

Apart from the odd festive variant ('Mr Kipling does make exceedingly merry mince pies'), the adverts stayed pretty much the same until 2001. Then came a 'rebranding exercise' and an advert which rocked the advertising world. Instead of a jolly Dickensian scene, the advert depicted a rather graphic Nativity play in which the Virgin Mary yells in pain as she gives birth to the baby Jesus. We later find that Mr Kipling is directing the play. The question is asked, 'Has Mr Kipling ever directed a play before?' The predictable answer is, 'No, but he does make exceedingly good cakes.' The advert was the subject of over 600 complaints and was pulled by Mr Kipling even before the Independent Television Commission could rule on it. Bad marketing or exceedingly good PR?

'Exceedingly good' and 'Mr Kipling' are so inextricably linked in our collective imagination that it is often hard for journalists or reviewers writing about the poet Rudyard Kipling to avoid using 'exceedingly good' at some point in their piece. Even the late folk-singer Peter Bellamy fell into the trap, calling his 1989 compilation of Kipling's poetry set to music *Rudyard Kipling Made Exceedingly Good Songs*.

full of Eastern promise

Fry's Turkish Delight

Fry's Turkish Delight has been advertised as being '**full of Eastern promise**' since 1957, although it was first launched in 1924, marketed as 'a mystical, exotic treat that lets you escape from the everyday'. Exactly what 'full of Eastern promise' means, apart from something vaguely strange and a bit naughty, is anybody's guess.

In the original TV advertisement, which featured a timeless jingle by Cliff Adams, a slave unrolled a carpet containing a glamorous female captive in front of an Eastern ruler and she began feeding him lumps of Turkish Delight which was, of course, said to be 'full of Eastern promise'. Over the years the term 'Eastern promise' has become a standard formula for conjuring up a Middle-Eastern or vaguely exotic atmosphere ('The skyline of mosques and palaces displays the city's Eastern promise').

The name of the product 'Turkish Delight' is amongst other things an ever so coy reference to the perceived carnal delights which travellers could once only enjoy in the non-Christian East, which began at the Turkish border. In modern multicultural Britain, it is not necessary to venture quite so far to enjoy these delights. A certain Mata Hari operating out of Worthing, Sussex, advertises her escort service with the words, 'Full of Eastern Promise – fancy something sweet? Let me be your Turkish Delight.'

I'm only here for the beer

Double Diamond

Since the 1950s, the popular slogan used to advertise Double Diamond beer had been 'Double Diamond works wonders', but in 1971 a new slogan came into being that quickly entered general usage: '**I'm only here for the beer**.'

Funnily enough for such an essentially English product, this new catchphrase was actually coined by an American advertising copywriter called Ros Levenstein, who happened to be working in Britain at the time. The concept behind the slogan was that the person speaking it was claiming to be a 'fun' person, more interested in enjoying a beer than taking part in whatever serious business was going on, and this was an idea that seemed to capture the public imagination at the time.

As with many slogans that become catchphrases, people who used it were often unaware of its origin (which is not necessarily good news for the advertisers). Who can say if the Duke of Edinburgh had Double Diamond in mind when he was quoted as saying at a champagne reception in late 1971, 'Don't look at me, I'm only here for the beer'?

In September 1973, a slightly altered form of the phrase was used in the *Sunday Times* magazine to headline an article about holidays in France: 'Only here for la bière'.

Is she or isn't she?

Harmony

An attractive young woman walks through the park on a sunny morning and is scrutinized by a couple of men. Nothing new there, you might think, but in 1978 the Harmony hairspray advert in which this incident was depicted really was something new. The innovative mild sexual innuendo of this advert has found a place in the nation's psyche and has led to the phrase '**Is she or isn't she?**' cropping up in some odd places.

The advertisement created a frisson by inducing the viewer to speculate about which particular sexual issue the men were arguing about. Whether she was wearing a bra? Whether she was pregnant? In the world of the advert it transpired that they were wondering whether her natural-looking hairstyle owed anything to the application of a hairspray, but in later years both of the other possibilities have been the subject of 'the Harmony question'.

A New Zealand fashion magazine began a feature on the Berlei One stitch-free bra ('a breakthrough in bra technology that gives wonderful shape yet looks and feels like you are wearing nothing') by asking the question 'Is she or isn't she?' But as the accompanying picture clearly showed that the 'she' in question *was* wearing a bra (and nothing else above the waist), the question might be considered somewhat redundant.

The Harmony question emerged in a rather different setting when the Japanese media went into a frenzy over signs that Crown Princess Masako might be pregnant and headlines asked, 'Is she or isn't she?' In the Harmony advert, the girl in the park had a can of hairspray jutting out of her bag to settle the question, but on this occasion Japan's Imperial Household Agency declined to comment.

It could be you

The National Lottery

Since its creation by John Major's government in 1994, Britain's National Lottery has rarely been out of the news. Although it has made over 2,000 people millionaires and raised £16 billion for over 180,000 different good causes, the Lottery has always been dogged by controversy. Alleged profiteering by Lottery operator Camelot, jackpot wins by convicted car-thieves and rapists, and the use of funds for such white elephants as the Millennium Dome and the National Centre for Popular Music in Sheffield (which closed after just sixteen months) have lost the Lottery some friends. Yet despite the bad press, the Lottery continues to rake in millions. Punters are still prepared to part with a pound, perhaps spurred on by the Lottery's first and most effective catchphrase, '**It could be you**.'

'It could be you' worked by stressing that someone was going to win the jackpot, and your chances were as good as anyone's. It chose not to stress the fact that the actual chances of your being the winner were about 14 million to one. The slogan established itself as a popular catchphrase, often being used to tempt people into some activity by dangling the prospect of success in front of them.

In 1998, however, the Lottery operator ditched the phrase, and there have followed a series of less successful slogans, starting with 'Maybe, just maybe', which perhaps reflected punters' growing acceptance that the odds of a major win were seriously stacked against them. Declining ticket sales resulted in a relaunch in 2002: the Lottery's name was changed to Lotto and £72 million was spent on an advertising campaign featuring Billy Connolly enjoining us, 'Don't live a little, live a Lotto' in a campaign that earned the unwanted award of 'Most Irritating Commercial of 2002'. More recently, we have been told to 'Think Lucky' in a campaign that features Fay Ripley as Lady Luck, alongside a purple-maned unicorn called Barry, voiced by comedian Graham Norton.

It's good to talk

British Telecom

In 1996 British Telecom was worried. Not about profits, perish the thought, but about the nation's mental health: we just weren't communicating enough. Our taciturnity concerned BT, who thought that it could save countless broken relationships if only it could get us to use the phone more often. So it launched a series of advertisements to remedy the situation, using Bob Hoskins as the instrument of its will. Hoskins, appearing to the TV audience but not to the tongue-tied people we saw in the adverts, demonstrated the importance of constant telephone dialogue. Looking on fondly as estranged relatives mended emotional fences on the phone, he reminded us at the end of each heart-warming tale that '**It's good to talk**.'

The adverts almost had the air of public information films, only they warned not of the hazards of flying kites near overhead power cables but of the calamitous consequences of not phoning your mum every night. The ubiquity of the BT ads meant that the phrase quickly became embedded in the British imagination. It was famously subverted by Jim Royle in the opening episode of *The Royle Family* (see page 133), and long after BT ditched the slogan, sub-editors are still able to pun on the words for comic effect. In 2001, for example, the BBC website ran a story about a parrot who had got his own e-mail account and was busy making friends all over the world. The headline: 'Parrot says: "It's good to squawk"'.

⇨ See also **ology**

I wouldn't give a Castlemaine XXXX for ...

Castlemaine XXXX

There are numerous phrases that speakers of English can use to indicate that they could not care less about something: besides not giving a damn, a toss, a hang or a rap, they can also fail to give a tinker's curse, a monkey's or even two hoots about it. Since 1986, they have also been able to say, '**I wouldn't give a Castlemaine XXXX for** it.'

Castlemaine XXXX – the second element of the name is pronounced 'four-ex' rather than 'kiss-kiss-kiss-kiss' – is an Australian beer brewed in Queensland. In the 1986 advertising campaign that launched the brand in Britain, the four repeated capital letters in the name were used as a gruff allusion to the F-word, echoing the coarse phrase 'I wouldn't give a f*** for ...', as British drinkers were assured that 'Australians wouldn't give a Castlemaine XXXX for anything else.' In fact, Castlemaine XXXX has been described as 'crisp, with a delicate aroma and sweet fruity taste', although presumably the macho Australian chaps in the adverts would break your jaw for offering this rather effete analysis of their drink of choice.

The use of XXXX in the name of the drink originally derived from the medieval European tradition of using Xs to indicate the strength of beer. This European tradition was brought to Australia by two Irishmen, Nicholas and Edwin Fitzgerald. They had arrived in Australia with their father Francis, a brewer, from the town of Castlemaine in Ireland – so called because of the nearby castle on the banks of the Maine River – and by the late 1880s had established Castlemaine as arguably Australia's first national beer brand.

Castlemaine celebrated its 125th birthday in October 2003. In 1999 it produced its five billionth 'stubby' (a stubby being a small bottle, approximately 250 millilitres in volume). We are told that, if placed end to end, five billion stubbies would form a line more than one million kilometres in length, stretching 27 times around the world. Alternatively, packaged in cartons and laid end to end, the same stubbies would form a 25-centimetre-high wall stretching about two and a quarter times around the world. Why anyone would want to attempt either feat is unclear.

110

Nice one, Cyril

Wonderloaf

Tottenham Hotspur has possibly been associated with more chart records than any other football team. Such classics as 'Tip Top Tottenham Hotspur' by the Totnamites, 'Diamond Lights' by Glenn and Chris, and 'Ossie's Dream' by Chas'n'Dave have delighted regulars at White Hart Line, if not music purists.

In 1973, the Cockerel Chorus got to number 14 with **'Nice one, Cyril'**, a jaunty tribute to the popular Spurs defender Cyril Knowles, although the song was not an original composition. It started off life in a commercial for Wonderloaf bread, directed by a young Alan Parker, in which a baker called Cyril takes credit for a particularly fine loaf (glossing over the fact that all Wonderloaf bread was mass-produced). Parker later found fame as the director of films such as *Midnight Express* and *The Commitments*, and he was not the only future celebrity associated with the commercial. The slogan 'Nice one, Cyril' was coined by Peter Mayle, who later wrote the bestselling travel book *A Year in Provence*.

You will not have seen Wonderloaf bread in the shops for many years, but the phrase 'Nice one, Cyril' lives on. It is still widely used to express approval, even to people who do not share their first name with the Wonderloaf baker or the old Spurs full-back.

ology
British Telecom

There is no shortage of spin-off books from TV series, but volumes based on commercials are pretty thin on the ground. However, one book that did emerge from an advertising campaign was *You Got an Ology?*, written by actress Maureen Lipman in 1989 in order to cash in on the success of her commercials for the newly privatized British Telecom.

Lipman appeared in a series of adverts playing a stereotypical Jewish grandmother called Beattie (Beattie ... BT ... get it?). In one of these she is shown talking on the phone to her grandson Anthony while preparing to send him a cake to celebrate his exam results. However, Anthony has failed most of his exams and has passed only one subject, sociology. Seeing a silver lining in this cloud, Beattie replies joyfully, 'An **ology**! He gets an ology and he says he's failed. You get an ology, you're a scientist!'

The word 'ology' was not invented by British Telecom or Maureen Lipman. Indeed, the word has been around since the 19th century when it was coined as a jocular term for any branch of science or knowledge. But the advert brought the word into wider use, besides opening up some money-spinning opportunities for its star.

⟹ See also **It's good to talk**

probably the best lager in the world
Carlsberg

Carlsberg's current advertising campaign states that its beer is 'so good the Danes hate to see it leave' – a slightly curious choice of words when one considers that all of the Carlsberg beer drunk in Britain is brewed in Northampton. Only time will tell if the phrase lasts as long as the Danish brewer's more famous slogan, '**probably the best lager in the world**'.

These words, first intoned in 1975 by gravelly-voiced Hollywood veteran Orson Welles, began Carlsberg's long-running campaign to get British drinkers to switch from warm bitter to cold lager. The adverts put across the message that Carlsberg is an upmarket kind of beer, an idea reinforced by the fact that Carlsberg brews by appointment to the Danish royal family. However, perhaps some 'brand contamination' has occurred in recent times. The brewer's extra-strength beer, Special Brew, was first produced in honour of Winston Churchill's visit to Denmark in 1950. Since then, though, it has become associated less with Britain's war leader and more with Britain's gentlemen of the road, the potent lager being popularly known as 'tramp fuel'.

Carlsberg's reputation as a brewer of fine lager may have been damaged by this, but the firm's classic slogan remains ingrained in British culture. It is now often adapted to things other than beer, so that the NSPCC can plug itself as 'probably the best charity advertiser in the world', while in 2003 *The Times* ran a glowing report on the Seychelles resort of Anse Volbert under the headline 'Probably the best beach in the world'.

reassuringly expensive
Stella Artois

Whoever it was who said that the adverts on TV are often better than the programmes might have had Stella Artois commercials in mind. High production values, large casts, and music from Verdi's *The Force of Destiny* combine to make Stella's witty homages to French art-house cinema some of the most admired adverts on television. Although each ad pastiches a different film or genre, they all drive home the message that Stella Artois beer is '**reassuringly expensive**'.

The Artois brewery in Belgium has been around since 1366, although production of lager beer did not start there until 1926. In an attempt to capture a large chunk of the premium lager market in Britain, Stella adopted the 'reassuringly expensive' slogan in 1981. The pastiches of Gallic cinema followed later, the first few being takeoffs of Claude Berri's 1986 films *Jean de Florette* and *Manon des sources*.

Stella's slogan has become part of the English language, and is often employed to describe a pricey product that considers itself to be a cut above its rivals. A recent article in *The Times*, for example, referred to the Range Rover as being 'understated but reassuringly expensive'.

refreshes the parts other beers cannot reach

Heineken

The British used to be a race of bitter and mild drinkers, but by the 1980s mild was a rarity in many regions and bitter had been eclipsed by lager as the UK's most popular pint. Advertising played a large role in altering the drinking habits of Britain's beer drinkers, changing the perception of lager from something women drank with a dash of lime to a drink that men were happy to imbibe with their friends. Heineken's clever and amusing adverts of the 1970s started the ball rolling, and their original slogan 'Heineken **refreshes the parts other beers cannot reach**' is still recognized today.

The phrase was created in 1974 and the first TV advert to use it involved a line of bare-footed policemen exhausted after a day pounding the beat. One of the bobbies is given a pint of the Dutch brew and immediately his toes start to wriggle. Victor Borge then supplies a voice-over with the slogan that is now a part of advertising history.

Although it is no longer used by Heineken, the phrase lives on in the advertising and marketing of other products. Digital television firm Telewest issued a press release in 2002 in which it told potential customers, 'If you're thinking of switching, or getting digital TV for the first time, you'd be bananas not to choose broadband cable. It refreshes the parts that satellite dishes and BT cannot reach.'

Even the Christian faith has invoked Heineken's slogan in order to spread the word of God, claiming that 'Traditional religion refreshes the parts schmaltzy liturgy cannot reach' and 'A sincere relationship with Jesus refreshes the inner parts other relationships simply cannot reach.'

tangoed

Tango

A controversial commercial from 1992 featured a man drinking a can of Tango. A slow-motion analysis then showed that more was afoot than just the consumption of orangeade. The replay revealed that at the moment the drinker took his sip, a rotund bald individual with bright orange skin had run up to him and slapped him firmly on the face. Two commentators, describing this assault as though reporting on a football match, explained that the shocked imbiber had just experienced the 'bite and buzz of real oranges'. The advert then concluded with the slogan 'You know when you've been **tangoed**.'

The commercial proved popular with children, some of whom took great delight in re-enacting the slapping scene with some vigour. Before long, doctors were noting an increased incidence of perforated eardrums, and the resultant outcry led to the orange gentleman replacing his trademark slap with a large kiss.

The word 'tangoed' has endured in British English, referring either to someone who has been hit by a sudden shock or to something that has taken on an unexpected orange tinge. When a section of a Nottingham canal became covered in orange sludge, for example, the BBC dusted off the expression and reported, 'City canal is "tangoed".'

In Ireland, meanwhile, the word has come to be used of the unnatural appearance that people can get as a result of the injudicious use of cosmetics: 'The job of any foundation is to give an appearance of flawless skin – not to dramatically alter its colour in order to give a tanned appearance, guaranteed only to make you look like you've been tangoed.'

That'll do nicely, sir

American Express

The American Express company built up its traveller's cheque and charge card business in the United States with the slogan 'Don't leave home without it!' (see page 102), but in the UK it is probably more readily associated with the slogan '**That'll do nicely, sir**.' In a culture where the settling of debts is a potential source of embarrassment, a jocular allusion to this phrase can often help to smooth over that awkward moment when money changes hands.

The slogan was used as the tagline for a series of advertisements in the 1970s and 1980s which portrayed the cheerful and enthusiastic welcome that awaited business travellers the minute they produced the company's characteristic green card. The adverts traded on this idea of exclusiveness, suggesting that owning an AmEx card would immediately mark one out as a member of an elite and privileged group – an image that stemmed from the fact that the card was aimed at well-heeled business travellers, requiring its users to pay a large annual fee and to settle their accounts in full each month, but offering a high level of service in return.

The campaign attracted a certain amount of mockery on the grounds that it appealed to snobbery and portrayed the people who accepted the card as servile flunkeys. It was famously sent up by the comedy show *Not the Nine O'Clock News* which ran a sketch in which a businessman found that using the card meant that not only did he receive a cheerful smile but the glamorous shop assistant (played by Pamela Stephenson) began unbuttoning her blouse and offering him sexual favours.

The man from Del Monte, he say, 'Yes!'

Del Monte

In a fruit grove in an unnamed developing country, a man wearing a Panama hat and a pristine white linen suit pauses by a tree and takes a bite out of a peach. Dozens of fruit pickers drop what they are doing and look on anxiously. Pleased by what he is eating, the elegantly dressed gent gives an affirmative nod to a nearby worker who shouts out delightedly, '**The man from Del Monte, he say, "Yes!"**'

This insight into the rather one-sided relationship between first-world companies and third-world growers might seem rather tasteless in the current era of fair-trade foods and ethical shopping. But before the welfare of primary producers became a consideration to shoppers, Del Monte was happy to portray itself as a remorselessly demanding taskmaster.

The adverts certainly made an impact, and Del Monte's slogan is still occasionally employed when the all-important decision of an authority figure is described. For example, the website Manchester Online alluded to it in this description of a referee declining to award a decision in favour of Dutch footballer Dennis Bergkamp: 'Bergkamp goes down. He say penalty. The man from Del Monte, he say, "No."'

va va voom

Renault Clio

Superstar French footballer Thierry Henry first became famous for his exploits on the soccer pitch, but he is now known to a wider audience through his adverts for the Renault Clio, in which he sings the praises of '**va va voom**', a somehow indefinable quality that is nevertheless instantly recognizable in sexy women, fancy cookery, cool jazz and fast cars.

The Clio adverts play on the supposed connection between French and everything chic, sexy and stylish, so when Henry asks, 'What's the French for "va va voom"?', we are intended to laugh and imagine that this expression is surely as Gallic as 'ooh la la'.

In fact the phrase originally comes from the mouth of a Greek car mechanic called Nick, who features in Robert Aldrich's 1955 film of Mickey Spillane's *Kiss Me Deadly* – a sweaty and brutal film noir whose plot centres on one of cinema's ultimate McGuffins – a box containing a deadly 'Great Whatsit' which you should *never* open (not on any account!). Mike Hammer, the thuggish anti-hero, has periodic chats with Nick, who has a habit of saying 'Va va voom!' to suggest the acceleration of a sports car, and life in the fast lane in general. When Nick comes to a sticky end, Hammer's regretful epitaph is, 'No more va va voom!'

Vorsprung durch Technik

Audi

Native speakers of English are notoriously bad at bothering to learn other languages. However, there are occasions when mass exposure through television has thrust a foreign phrase into the limelight, and so it is that the German phrase '**Vorsprung durch Technik**', the motto of the Audi car company, has become familiar to English speakers.

The phrase (which means literally 'progress through technology') has been used as the tagline to Audi's British advertising campaigns since 1984, when it was first voiced by the lugubrious Geoffrey Palmer. The adverts played on the stereotype that German car manufacturing was synonymous with quality, whereas British mass car production was anything but. The use of the German motto reinforced the idea that these cars were of a completely different order to the ones that Audi's British competitors might be trying to sell you.

The high-risk tactic of using words from a foreign language for the purpose of advertising proved highly successful. *Vorsprung durch Technik* is now probably the best-known of all German phrases for many English speakers, and it is often loosely applied to express the idea of superior quality German engineering.

It was even incorporated into song lyrics by two of the leading bands of the 1990s: you can hear it on the title tracks of U2's album *Zooropa* and Blur's *Parklife* (both released in 1994). The allure of the phrase for popular musicians was seen again in 1998, when German trance DJ Paul van Dyk released an album called *Vorsprung Dyk Technik*.

Whassup?

Budweiser

Budweiser beer's advertising campaign of 2000 was either amusing and innovative or deeply annoying, depending on your perspective. It launched a catchphrase, '**Whassup?**', which drunken young men were only too keen to imitate, and which for a while became almost as common a greeting as 'Hello'.

The advert featured four young African-American men speaking to one another on the phone. They all used the greeting 'Whassup?' (What's up?), with each new rendition being even more mannered than the previous one. The anticlimactic answer to the enquiry – which turned out to make much less of an impression than the question itself – was 'Watching the game, having a Bud.'

The advert originated as a short film that had nothing at all to do with beer. Charles Stone III created a two-minute film that consisted of himself and his three Philadelphian friends saying 'Whassup?' over and over again. Called *True* (also later to be used as a Budweiser slogan), the piece came to the attention of Budweiser's advertising agency, who liked it and ended up using the four friends in their advert.

The campaign won a number of awards and the advert spawned some imitators on the Internet, most notably a Lancastrian pastiche in which 'Ey up!' replaces the original slogan.

You are really spoiling us

Ferrero Rocher

'The Ambassador's receptions are noted in society for their host's exquisite taste that captivates his guests.' With these words began one of the most talked about adverts of the 1990s. By the time the campaign was dropped in 1999, it had spawned numerous parodies and created a catchphrase which is sometimes used literally but more often ironically: **'You are really spoiling us.'**

The commercial, used by Ferrero Rocher to advertise its chocolate-and-hazelnut sweets, revolved around an 'Ambassador's reception'. In the embassy, a butler glided around with a pyramid of chocolates on a silver platter while the cosmopolitan guests expressed delight at the sweets and respect for the Ambassador's good taste. One glamorous female guest even remarked, 'Monsieur, with these chocolates you are really spoiling us!'

With the inept dubbing and unconvincing dialogue, it all seemed like a pastiche of the worst adverts from the 1970s. The product was portrayed as sophisticated and exclusive, yet it was inexpensive and common as muck: corner shops and garages stocked Ferrero Rocher. Yet, precisely because it was so awful, the advert achieved cult status in Britain. Themed parties were based around it and a DJ called Ferrolicious released a single, sampling dialogue from the ad, called 'The Ambassador's Party'. The single didn't achieve much, but the advert stayed on our screens for four years until it was replaced by one that featured neither the Ambassador nor the pyramid. Fans were outraged and started a campaign for its return. The clamour was partially successful in that a similar advert appeared in 2003, but this one was noticeably less naff and featured an ambassadress rather than an ambassador.

PART TWO

Make it so
Star Trek: The Next Generation

When TV executives decided to create a follow-up to the classic science-fiction series *Star Trek* (see page 174) in 1987, it fell to British Shakespearean actor Patrick Stewart to play the new captain of the *Enterprise*, Jean-Luc Picard. The character of Picard is quite a contrast with the all-action, high-kicking, more-balls-than-a-Christmas-tree James Kirk, played by William Shatner in the original series. Picard is something of a 24th-century Renaissance man, with an interest in archaeology and music, a strong sense of duty and a preference for diplomacy over combat.

However, this does not make him a soft touch, and his firm leadership style is epitomized by the catchphrase '**Make it so**', his usual reply to any suggestion with which he agrees. It sums up neatly his decisiveness and 'get-on-and-do-it' attitude. Often the words are addressed to his capable second-in-command or 'Number One' (Commander Riker, played by Jonathan Frakes), or to the ship's chief engineer Geordi La Forge (played by LeVar Burton).

As well as becoming familiar to the legions of *Star Trek* fans, the catchphrase has been picked up by management gurus, who are always on the lookout for a new mantra and have been attracted by its succinctness. It was even used as the title for a management book on leadership lessons that can be learned from *Star Trek*.

Although Picard is meant to be French (raised on the family farm in Labarre, and apparently named after the French oceanographer Jacques Picard), there is not the slightest hint of a Gallic accent when he delivers his curt instruction. Creator of the programme Gene Roddenberry had originally insisted that a French actor should play the part but was won over by the sonorous vowels of this son of York.

Manolos
⇨ See **Cosmopolitan**

125

marmalize

The Ken Dodd Show

Ken Dodd popularized the word 'diddy' through his Diddymen characters on his television shows from the 1960s onwards (see page 41), but his influence on English vocabulary does not stop there. He is also responsible for popularizing the word '**marmalize**', through his creation of Mick the Marmalizer, the psychopathic Diddyman who greeted allcomers with the words, 'I'll marmalize yer!'

The word 'marmalize' has now found its way into dictionaries under various spellings, but with general agreement that it means 'to thrash, defeat heavily, destroy, etc'. The derivation of the word seems to lie in a fusion of some or all of the words 'murder', 'pulverize' and 'marmalade'. Presumably the idea is of energetically reducing one's opponent to marmalade or an equivalent condition.

Ken Dodd's fertile imagination and his zest for word creation have also enriched the English language in other ways. He is particularly associated with the term '**tattifilarious**', which suggests a rough equivalence with 'hilarious', and is one of many nonsense words (others include 'discumknockerated' and 'plumptiousness') with which he peppers his surreal stage ramblings.

Then there is also the **tickling stick**, a feather duster to you and me, but in Doddy's hands the sceptre that the King of Comedy brandishes as he regally reduces his diddy subjects to helpless fits.

massive

⇨ See **Booyakasha!**

meanwhile back at the ranch ...

Bonanza

The phrase '**meanwhile back at the ranch ...**' is often used when people who have been giving an account of exciting or exotic adventures want to indicate a transition to a more familiar domestic scene. This popular catchphrase goes back to the change-of-scene captions that accompanied silent movies, but it is forever associated with the goings-on at one ranch in particular, *The Ponderosa*, home of the Cartwright family in the long-running Western series *Bonanza*.

Bonanza, which ran from 1959 to 1973, saw the Cartwright family survive just about every storyline possible in the horse-opera genre. Ben, the grizzled patriarch widower (played by Lorne Greene), dispensed fatherly wisdom to his three very different sons: dark and brooding Adam (Pernell Roberts), big and affable Hoss (Dan Blocker) and handsome young rebel Little Joe (Michael Landon).

The show's opening credits were unmistakeable, with its trademark Western theme belting out over shots of a map of Nevada which somewhat inexplicably goes on fire to allow our heroes to gallop towards the camera through the resulting singed aperture.

The ranch setting proved an ideal one for a television series, giving as it did a constant framework around which countless story variations could be woven, and allowing innumerable guest stars to come and go. Indeed, the formula was so successful that it was copied by later cowboy series such as *The Virginian* and *The High Chaparral*.

mission impossible

Mission: Impossible

Whether it is attempting to eliminate drugs from inner-city neighbourhoods or trying get a straight answer from a politician, any task that apparently cannot be achieved may be referred to as '**mission impossible**'.

The phrase is taken from the title of the long-running American espionage series *Mission: Impossible*. This programme ran in the States from 1966 to 1973 and featured the Impossible Mission Taskforce, a team of government spies and specialists who were assigned apparently impossible missions that in fact turned out to be well within their compass. The original series featured team leader Dan Briggs (played by Steven Hill), but from the second series the leading character was the silver-haired Jim Phelps (Peter Graves). Among the supporting cast were Leonard Nimoy and Martin Landau, who successively took on the role of the team's resident master of disguise.

In each episode of the series, the team would receive its mission from the mysterious 'Secretary' in the form of a tape. The tape would always exhort the team to action with the words 'Your mission, should you choose to accept it, is …' and then conclude with 'This tape will self-destruct in five seconds', after which time smoke would start to emerge from the tape recorder, providing a cue for the opening titles to begin.

The phrase '**This tape will self-destruct in five seconds**' has been much imitated as a warning of an imminent demise, re-emerging in such unlikely forms as 'This party will self-destruct in five minutes', 'My offer to you will self-destruct in five days' and 'The actors in this show will self-destruct in five episodes'.

mole
Tinker, Tailor, Soldier, Spy

It is now quite normal to hear the word '**mole**' used to refer to a person who infiltrates an organization and passes secret information to contacts outside it. Like the burrowing animals of the same name, human moles are adept at penetrating deeply and remaining concealed for long periods.

Yet this use of the word was quite unfamiliar to most English speakers until John Le Carré's novel *Tinker, Tailor, Soldier, Spy* was televised in 1979. In this adaptation, Alec Guinness played the central character of George Smiley, a veteran spy brought out of retirement to track down a 'mole' operating within British intelligence. In the course of seven episodes of complex plotting and often impenetrable dialogue, Guinness carved out a definitive portrayal of a British spy and won a BAFTA award for himself in the process.

Le Carré peppered his story with arcane jargon, and so viewers of the series became accustomed to hearing agents having apparently nonsensical conversations about 'Control', 'the Circus', 'babysitters' and 'lamplighters'. Some of this jargon was invented by Le Carré (who was amused to learn that it was soon imitated by real-life operatives). The term 'mole', however, was borrowed from the jargon of Soviet agents, who had been using the word (or rather its Russian equivalent, *krot*) since the 1920s.

Television found another use for the term in 2000 when Australia's Seven Network launched a game show called *The Mole.* The premise of this show (which also spawned short-lived versions in Britain and America) was that one of the contestants was a plant inserted by the production crew to sabotage the genuine contestants' chances of winning.

mondo
⇨ See **Cowabunga!**

129

Monty Python's Flying Circus

Before the arrival on our screens in 1969 of *Monty Python's Flying Circus* there was little continuity between the sketches in TV comedy shows. Each skit was usually a distinct entity that had a beginning, a middle, and an end that finished with a punchline. The Pythons broke this rule to glorious effect, with sketches weaving in and out of one another, stopping abruptly, or segueing into surreal cartoons. Although it poked fun at many British institutions, the show was much more surreal than satirical, and this explains the timelessness and longevity of such sketches as 'The Fish-Slapping Dance', 'The Ministry of Silly Walks' and 'The Lumberjack Song'.

American cartoonist Terry Gilliam and Oxbridge graduates John Cleese, Graham Chapman, Eric Idle, Michael Palin and Terry Jones had worked on programmes such as *Do Not Adjust Your Set* and *At Last the 1948 Show* in the 1960s. They were brought together into a team by Barry Took and wrote and performed four series for the BBC (the last of which was Cleeseless) between 1969 and 1974 and also collaborated on four feature films.

The Pythons' popularity is still huge. Their many fans know some of the sketches word for word and the adjective '**Pythonesque**' has become firmly established in the English language to describe humour that approximates to their template. However, we might have been using a different word to describe surreal and bizarre humour had the team chosen a different name for their sketch show. 'Owlish', 'Megapodic' or 'Stoatesque' could just as easily have entered our lexicon had the show been named *Owl Stretching Time*, *Arthur Megapode's Cheap Show* or *The Year of the Stoat* instead. These alternative titles, along with a number of others, were put forward and rejected before the cast and crew finally settled on *Monty Python's Flying Circus*.

Not only has the name of the programme become established in the language, but several catchphrases introduced by the show have, through long and reverent repetition, also become part of the fabric of English.

People who wish to invoke the spirit of the Pythons may well introduce a new subject by saying, '**And now for something**

completely different.' Eric Idle first uttered these words in the Pythons' debut programme in 1969, but the words are particularly associated with John Cleese's performances as the show's continuity announcer. Whether wearing a bikini, roasting on a spit or sitting behind a desk in a zoo cage, Cleese would keep a straight face and use this line to link one surreal sketch to the next. The phrase became synonymous with the programme and was used as the title of the Pythons' 1971 feature film, a 'best of' compilation of sketches from the TV shows.

Another much repeated expression came from the popular 'Spanish Inquisition' sketch. Cardinals Ximinez, Biggles and Fang were a running joke throughout one particular episode, appearing first when a worker, frustrated at his attempts to communicate to an aristocratic woman that there was 'trouble at t'mill', registered his despair at her high-handed interrogation with the words '**I didn't expect the Spanish Inquisition**.' The trio then appeared suddenly, with Ximinez (played by Michael Palin) proclaiming triumphantly, 'Nobody expects the Spanish Inquisition!' To this day, the sketch is apt to be quoted when a person wishes to suggest that a line of questioning has been pursued to excess.

Without doubt, however, the most famous of all the *Python* sketches is 'The Parrot Sketch'. Cleese and Palin intended to satirize the often woeful levels of customer care in Britain in the 1970s with this tale of a man complaining to a pet shop owner about the death of a parrot he had just bought. The shop owner tries to sidestep the issue with remarks about the bird's plumage and insists that the parrot is only resting. The angry customer, played by Cleese, finally snaps and delivers a tirade proclaiming his certainty about the parrot's death, in which he rattles off an astonishing variety of synonyms for 'dead', culminating in the line '**This is an ex-parrot**.' In the late 1980s the joke was adapted by one of Margaret Thatcher's speech writers and used by the then Prime Minister to declare the Social Democratic Party to be an 'ex-party'. Roughly a decade later, it was the turn of the Conservative Party to suffer adverse fortunes, and *The Sun* jumped on the dead-parrot bandwagon, delivering an editorial proclaiming William Hague's Tories to be an 'ex-party'.

muppet
The Muppet Show

The Muppets are a group of furry characters created by the American puppeteer Jim Henson. They have appeared in the educational programme *Sesame Street*, in various feature films and, most memorably, in their own series *The Muppet Show* (1976–81), winning the affection of millions of people all over the world.

The Muppets were a big hit in Britain too, yet the British uniquely also use the word '**muppet**' as a term of abuse meaning 'a foolish or stupid person'. Such is its power in British English that Arsenal footballer Ian Wright was red-carded in a match in 1994 for calling referee Robert Hart a muppet.

Ian Wright was certainly not the first person to take the Muppets' name in vain. The word has been used in Britain for many years, especially as an item of prison slang, suggesting that a person's mental faculties are on a par with those of a glove puppet. It was probably first recorded on celluloid in Mike Leigh's 1983 film *Meantime*. Depicting the dreary lives of a family living in a London council estate, Leigh's comedy focuses on the relationship between two brothers, Mark (Phil Daniels) and Colin (Tim Roth). Mark is intelligent and sarcastic, relentlessly taunting his somewhat retarded brother and addressing him as 'muppet' rather than using his name.

As the term has become more widely used, it has lost some of its force and it can now be used in a vaguely self-deprecating way, as when England rugby player Steve Thompson recently told the *Daily Telegraph*, 'To be honest [my friends] think I'm a bit of a muppet. A muppet that's won the World Cup, though.'

Quite how Kermit the Frog, Miss Piggy and the rest of the Muppets feel about this usage is not recorded.

... my arse!

The Royle Family

When *The Royle Family* first aired on British television in September 1998, many viewers did not know what to make of the programme and mistook the low-key comedy series for another fly-on-the-wall documentary. However, the opening line of that first episode, 'Ninety-eight quid! Ninety-eight quid! "It's good to talk", my arse!', set the tone for the 18 shows and two Christmas specials that followed.

Whether, as here, complaining about the telephone bill or railing against the excesses of his wife Barbara (Sue Johnston) or the foolishness of his son Antony (Ralf Little), the expletive '**my arse!**' was never far from the lips of the father of the house Jim Royle (Ricky Tomlinson). The show, written by Caroline Aherne and Craig Cash (who also starred as the Royles' daughter Denise and her partner Dave), was set in the front room of a working-class northern English family who spend most of their time watching television. The casting of Johnston and Tomlinson was a neat touch as they were already familiar to British viewers as husband and wife Bobby and Sheila Grant from the soap opera *Brookside* (see page 24).

Slovenly and unkempt – the clothes that he wore were not washed once during the filming of the three series – and rarely budging from his armchair, Jim could be relied on to apply the 'my arse!' label of disapproval at least once a show. Over the years it was appended to such diverse items as Dale Winton, feng shui, Bermuda, makeovers, balloons, the millennium, Christmas Day, Anne Robinson, bidets, sheep and pasta. His penchant for scatological turns of phrase also meant that his family and the audience were kept informed of his bowel movements with references to going for a 'Tom Tit' or 'Eartha Kitt', visiting the well-known Arab 'Mustapha Crap', and the appearance of a 'turtlehead' in his pants.

Jim Royle's coarse catchphrase was not original – in 1995, for example, the Irish poet Brendan Kennelly had published a book of verse entitled *Poetry My Arse*. However, the huge popularity of *The Royle Family* has given it a wider appeal. Ricky Tomlinson himself exploited this with a DVD of his stand-up comedy entitled *Laughter My Arse!* and a CD called *Music My Arse!* (featuring his accomplished banjo playing), and it has also been used for the title of a book debunking diets (*Diet ... My Arse*).

Mysteron

Captain Scarlet and the Mysterons

Even if you had never watched television, you could probably guess that the **Mysterons** would have to be either a group of enigmatic bad guys or else a 1960s beat combo. In fact, they are the former, part of a distinguished tradition of similar-sounding extraterrestrial threats that includes the Mekons (*Dan Dare*), the Klingons (*Star Trek*) and the Vogons (*The Hitchhiker's Guide to the Galaxy*).

The Mysterons were the baddies in the 1967 puppet drama *Captain Scarlet and the Mysterons*, one of several popular children's adventure series that Gerry and Sylvia Anderson produced using a process they dubbed 'Supermarionation'. (Others included *Stingray*, *Fireball XL5* and *Thunderbirds*.)

The premise of the series, played out over 32 episodes, is that an elite group called Spectrum is leading the defence of the Earth against a war of terror being conducted from Mars by the Mysterons. The Mysterons' chief weapon is a regeneration process known as 'retro-metabolism', which they use to destroy and then replicate selected Earthlings. The heroic Captain Scarlet is made a Mysteron agent in the first episode, but their hold on him is broken and the regeneration process renders him indestructible, a quality he often requires in subsequent episodes.

The Mysterons themselves are seen only as rings of light that wander across the set to the accompaniment of spooky music. It is said that the Mysterons are invisible not just for budgetary reasons, but because Gerry Anderson wanted to avoid appearing wrong should life ever be discovered on Mars. The advantage the Mysterons hold through being invisible is somewhat diminished by their insistence on announcing their sinister intentions at the beginning of each episode rather than striking without warning. No wonder they keep getting beaten.

⮕ See also **SIG**

naff
⮕ See **Porridge**

name that tune
Name That Tune

If you are certain of your ability to identify something, whether it be an actor, a rare breed of dog or the capital of a far-flung country, you might confidently assert that you can **name that tune**.

A US musical-knowledge quiz show with the title *Name That Tune* ran in various incarnations from 1953 to 1981, but UK viewers were first made familiar with the phrase when it was used as the title of a segment of the 1970s ITV variety show *Wednesday at Eight*. It emerged as a UK game show in its own right in 1983 and ran until 1987, hosted first by chuckling Liverpool comic Tom O'Connor and later by variety icon Lionel Blair, and employing sultry Maggie Moone as the resident singer. A hipper, glossier version of the show, hosted by doyen of authentic cool Jools Holland, returned for a year on Channel Five in 1998.

The 1980s show had several rounds, including 'Song and Singer' and 'Roulette Wheel', but it is the eponymous 'Name that Tune' round that most people remember. In it, two contestants compete to identify a tune after hearing only a very few of the opening notes, the precise number of notes being chosen by the contestant and declared in a 'bid' using the formula 'I'll name that tune in five/four/three, etc', with this musical Dutch auction continuing until one contestant's nerve broke.

As a result of the popularity of the programme, the phrase 'I'll name that tune in one' has become familiar as a waggish response to a sudden and unexpected noise of any kind, such as the smash of tableware on a kitchen floor or an eruption of sound from either end of a drinking companion.

Nay, nay, and thrice nay
⇨ See **Titter ye not!**

135

Neighbours

In 1987, Michael Grade, then controller of BBC1, was pestered by his daughter to move an Australian soap opera called *Neighbours*, which the BBC had tucked away quietly in its early-morning and lunchtime schedules, to a time when she and her friends were not at school. Grade was impressed at the interest the show had generated among the younger generation and moved it to a more accessible tea-time slot. What he could not have forecast was that within months the programme would become one of the most avidly viewed on British television and would play a key role in changing the way that young people speak.

Neighbours was created by Reg Watson, a television producer who had previously worked in Britain on the soap opera *Crossroads*. Having returned to his native Australia, he was eager to develop a new Australian soap based on the formula established by *Crossroads* and *Coronation Street*. What he came up with was a series centred around the residents of Ramsay Street, a cul-de-sac in the fictional Melbourne suburb of Erinsborough. The show had various working titles, including *One Way Street* and *No Through Road*, but was eventually broadcast under the title *Neighbours* in March 1985. The show's original broadcaster, Channel Seven, was disappointed with the audience ratings and decided to axe it, at which point it was taken up by the rival Channel Ten, where it was revamped using younger actors and glossier production values. It never looked back and established itself as a global success that launched the careers of a number of international stars, including Kylie Minogue, Jason Donovan, Guy Pearce and Natalie Imbruglia.

The runaway success that *Neighbours* achieved in Britain paved the way for other Australian soaps – most notably *Home and Away* – to be shown at peak viewing times. With so much Australian English being heard in Britain's living rooms, it is not surprising that many items of Australian vernacular came to be adopted in British English. Not only this, but the characteristic rising intonation of Australian English – which tends to make every sentence sound as though it is a question – was also widely imitated by young people in Britain and has now become commonplace.

A *Neighbours* glossary

arvo	*afternoon*
bikie	*a member of a motorcycle gang*
Buckley's	*no chance*
chocker	*very full*
dag	*an unattractive girl or woman*
daggy	*unfashionable and unattractive*
dero	*a homeless person*
dob someone in	*to inform on or betray someone*
drongo	*a stupid person*
go off at	*to scold or reprimand*
journo	*a journalist*
mongrel	*a despicable person*
muso	*a musician*
oldies	*parents*
pash	*to engage in amorous behaviour*
perv at	*to look at lustfully*
rack off!	*go away!*
rage	*to party*
rapt	*delighted*
rellie	*a relative*
spunk	*an attractive boy or man*
uni	*university*
wowser	*a spoilsport*

nerk
Porridge

The classic prison-based comedy *Porridge* (see page 150) popularized a number of slang words in its attempt to steer a middle way between authentic prison argot and acceptable language for family viewing.

A prime example of this is the use of '**nerk**' – or 'nurk' as it was written in the original scripts – as the term of choice to describe a foolish or annoying person. The term is a convenient substitute for the similar-sounding slang word 'berk', which is itself a euphemism for a much stronger expletive, 'berk' being a short form of 'Berkshire hunt' which is Cockney rhyming slang for the C-word.

> "What's wrong with you nurks in here? Can't you see when a man wants to be left alone?"

The word 'nerk' itself is first recorded in the 1950s, and seems to derive from the name 'Fred Nerk' which, in the 1950s, was used a personification of stupidity, probably drawing on the associations of 'nerd' and 'berk'. Indeed, the name Fred Nerk was often used by Harry Secombe as an idiotic character in his 1950s comedy shows.

nice little earner
⇨ See **Arthur Daley**

Nice to see you, to see you nice
⇨ See **The Generation Game**

not a lot

Odd One Out

The magician and comedian Paul Daniels has had a long career on
television and his catchphrase from the earliest days has been 'You'll
like it. **Not a lot**, but you'll like it.' This phrase has been frequently
mimicked to the point where if you ask anyone how they like
something it is now almost inevitable that you will receive the reply
'Not a lot.'

Daniels was born in 1938 in Middlesbrough, and his big break came
in 1970 when he came second in a programme of the *Opportunity
Knocks* series. This soon led to an appearance on the *Wheeltappers
and Shunters Social Club*, a variety programme staged as if being
performed in an old-fashioned working men's club. His blend of
skilful magic and amusing banter made him one of the most popular
entertainers of the period.

In the 1980s and 1990s Daniels established himself as a frontman
on a number of game shows, and as the host of *Odd One Out* his
catchphrase became familiar to a national audience. Similar roles in
Every Second Counts and *Wipe Out* ensured that his face and voice
have become among the best-known on British television.

So the next time that you ask someone how they like something and
they reply 'Not a lot', you'll know that Paul Daniels is to blame.

now then, now then

⇨ See **How's about that, then?**

nul points

Eurovision Song Contest

'**Nul points**' (to be said with a French accent, a bit like *nool pwang*) is the designation reserved for the very worst losers and non-starters, as in 'Royaume-Uni, nul points'. Loosely translated, this means not just 'United Kingdom, no points' but something more like 'United Kingdom, no points: hahahahahahahaha' – at least, this is what it appeared to mean in Riga, Latvia, when the UK's 2003 *Eurovision Song Contest* entry 'Cry Baby' by Jemini disastrously failed to score.

The Gallic nature of the phrase comes from the custom that announcements in the annual songfest are made first in French and then in English, so that the French tends to convey the message, and the English gets lost in the consequent applause or guffaws.

Jemini's song wasn't a masterpiece, but the sound monitors weren't working properly on the night, and the UK had just sided with George W Bush over the invasion of Iraq while the rest of Europe conspicuously had not. The result offered ample ammunition to those who believe that Eurovision voting has more to do with political points-scoring than musical performance.

However, given that all it takes to score a point is for a single participating country to nominate your song among the best ten, not scoring any points at all is quite a difficult feat to achieve. But Jemini were not the first: others who managed it have included Switzerland's Gunvor singing 'Lass Ihn' (Birmingham, 1998); Norway's Tor Endresen singing 'San Francisco' (Dublin, 1997); Lithuania's Ovidijus Vysniauskas singing 'Lopsine Mylimai' (Dublin, 1994); and Austria's Thomas Forstner singing 'Venedig im Regen' (Rome, 1991).

ocker
The Mavis Bramston Show

An '**ocker**' is a stereotypically boorish and unsophisticated Australian male, the kind of bloke who sits in bars scratching his crotch and belching while attempting to drink his own body weight in lager. Although the term is quite well known outside Australia, few people in the northern hemisphere realize that it is a relatively recent invention inspired by a television programme. In fact, the character of Ocker – a traditional Aussie form of the name Oscar – was created by the comedians Ron Frazer and Barry Creyton for a series of sketches on *The Mavis Bramston Show*, a satirical programme that ran on Australia's Channel Seven from 1964 to 1968.

In the sketches Frazer and Creyton portrayed a couple of hard-drinking types called Jack and Ocker who exchanged their provincial bar-room wisdom in broad Aussie tones. From this caricature, the idea of the ocker took root in the Australian consciousness.

Although the idea of the ocker is essentially bound up with typically male behaviour, the term managed to leap the gender divide in the 1970s, when a certain brand of brash Aussie woman came to be known as an 'ockerina'.

Oh my God!
⇨ See **Friends**

Oh my God, they killed Kenny!
⇨ See **South Park**

141

Only Fools and Horses

In 2004, BBC viewers voted *Only Fools and Horses* Britain's favourite sitcom. To deny the top spot to such classics as *Fawlty Towers*, *Blackadder* and *Porridge* was no mean feat for a show whose first series in 1981 drew only mediocre ratings. But instead of cancelling *Only Fools*, the BBC gave it another chance. The show rewarded the Corporation with steadily climbing viewing figures which culminated in a peak of 24.3 million for the final of a trilogy of Christmas specials in 1996. These were staggering ratings for a show competing in the multi-channel and satellite era.

Only Fools and Horses, written by John Sullivan, concerns the dodgy dealings of cocky market trader Derek 'Del Boy' Trotter (David Jason) and his more studious but less self-assured younger brother Rodney (Nicholas Lyndhurst). They live in a council flat in the high-rise Nelson Mandela Towers, from which they run their business empire, Trotter's Independent Traders. Many episodes revolve around get-rich-quick schemes which Del launches into with the confident prediction 'This time next year we'll be millionaires.'

Although the show had its fair share of slapstick humour, there was also a great deal of warmth and depth. The use of actors rather than stand-up comics enabled the show to tackle serious subjects such as the miscarriage suffered by Rodney's partner Cassandra and the deaths of the Trotters' two elderly relatives, Grandad and Uncle Albert. The tensions arising from living in a confined space with family members from whom one cannot escape was another rich source of comedy. This territory was familiar to viewers from *Steptoe and Son* (see page 220), but whereas the Steptoes' relationship was characterized by bitterness and resentment, the Trotters, despite the odd falling-out, were held together by genuine affection.

The show's setting in the Peckham district of south London allowed writer John Sullivan to flavour his scripts with a number of his favourite local words and phrases. Del Boy frequently called his younger sibling a '**plonker**' (see page 148) and a '**dipstick**' (see page 42) when things went wrong. On the other hand, when things were going his way, he was prone to express his contentment with two interjections: '**cushty**' and '**lovely jubbly**'. 'Cushty' has a colonial derivation, being British soldiers' slang for Cushtabar, a town in India considered to be an easy posting. The origin of 'lovely jubbly' is closer to home: it was the slogan used by an orange soft drink John Sullivan remembered from his childhood in the 1950s. Both of these expressions have become popular. (In recent years, 'lovely jubbly' has also come to be associated with TV's 'Naked Chef' Jamie Oliver (see page 153), and it even appears in a glossary of terms he compiled for the benefit of American fans who struggled to understand his London vernacular.)

Another source of linguistic humour was Del Boy's penchant for sprinkling his speech with foreign words and phrases he didn't really understand. His favourite French word was *bonjour*, but its ability to make his speech sound more sophisticated was somewhat undermined by the fact that he thought it meant 'goodbye' rather than 'hello'. He also claimed to speak German, although the only phrase he could manage was *Vorsprung durch Technik*.

Even the name '**Del Boy**' itself has come to be widely used in British English as a useful shorthand for a resourceful wheeler-dealer with an aversion to paying VAT. In 2000, for example, Consumer Affairs Minister Kim Howells made a speech saying that people should abandon their sentimental image of a Del Boy selling counterfeit designer clothes, football strips, perfumes, CDs and videos and realize that buyers of fake goods were in fact helping to finance drug gangs, terrorists and international racketeers.

Ooh, Betty

Some Mothers Do 'Ave 'Em

Some Mothers Do 'Ave 'Em, which was first broadcast in 1973, was one of the most popular sitcoms ever made by the BBC. Written by Raymond Allen, it detailed the disastrous domestic and working life of Frank Spencer (Michael Crawford). Spencer was a timid and ineffectual man incapable of doing the simplest thing without making a mess of it. The resulting calamities were often memorable in that they required the leading man to perform dangerous and elaborate stunts. Crawford spurned the use of a stuntman and delighted viewers with bravura displays of physical comedy reminiscent of the likes of Buster Keaton and Harold Lloyd.

As well as his infallible ability to bring disaster to any situation, Spencer was noted for his trademark raincoat and beret, an outfit that made him an easy target for impressionists. The tremulous and apologetic delivery employed by Crawford for the character was also much imitated, as were his catchphrases. '**Ooh, Betty**' was the phrase Frank used to summon help from or explain his latest mishap to his long-suffering wife (played by Michelle Dotrice), while a '**whoopsie**' was Frank's nursery word for something the cat might do in his beret.

Frank Spencer remains one of British comedy's most easily recognizable and frequently impersonated characters, even among people who were not even born when *Some Mothers Do 'Ave 'Em* ended in 1978. In 2003 a Sussex newspaper reported the tale of a 21-year-old charity worker who found a police radio at a petrol station and proceeded to broadcast his Frank Spencer impressions, flooding the police channel with phrases such as 'Ooh, Betty'. When he was eventually stopped by traffic police, he greeted them in the style of Michael Crawford's character with the words 'Can I help you, officers?'

pass

⇨ See **I've started so I'll finish**

peeps

Saturday Live

Before Harry Enfield found nationwide fame with Loadsamoney (see page 94), he launched his television career on *Saturday Live* with a character called Stavros, a friendly kebab shop owner with a unique take on the English language. Stavros dispensed observations on life in an accent that was part Hellenic, part Hackney. His words frequently became mangled but nevertheless managed to retain a certain poetic charm, and this close observation of the speech patterns of recent Greek immigrants made Enfield's character a hit with audiences. Indeed, Enfield based Stavros on an actual person: Adam Athanaffiou, the owner of a Greek takeaway in the area of London where the comedian and his writing partner Paul Whitehouse shared a flat.

Stavros's best-known coinage was '**peeps**', a diminutive of 'people'. It is still used to this day as a form of address in informal British English, a testament to the popularity of Britain's favourite kebab shop owner.

Saturday Live was a late-night comedy show that first broadcast in 1985 on Channel 4. It showcased the talents of many of the new generation of comedians, including Rik Mayall, Adrian Edmondson, Dawn French and Jennifer Saunders. Ben Elton hosted the show and Stephen Fry and Hugh Laurie were regulars. Yet veteran comics also got a look-in, with both Peter Cook and Frankie Howerd finding a new audience through the programme. But *Saturday Live* is most notable for giving Harry Enfield his big break. When it started he was an unknown, but by the time the show transferred to Friday nights a few years later, he had become one of its main attractions.

perfick
The Darling Buds of May

A catchphrase can sometimes be a double-edged sword, turning an actor or comedian into a household name one day, but becoming impossible to shake off after it has done its work. Catherine Zeta Jones was haunted for much of the 1990s not by a catchphrase but by a single word. In a recent interview the actress recalled that there was a time when she would walk down the street and everyone would shout '**perfick**'. At first she would smile through gritted teeth and give a friendly wave, but after a while, she recalls, 'I really felt like saying, "Look, piss off."'

'Perfick' is a Kentish pronunciation of 'perfect' and became a national buzzword between 1991 and 1993 through ITV's adaptation of H E Bates' *The Darling Buds of May*. Starring David Jason, Pam Ferris and Catherine Zeta Jones, this whimsical drama set in 1950s Kent concerned the bucolic adventures of the tax-dodging Larkin family. David Jason played the head of the family, Pop Larkin, who habitually expressed approval by declaring things to be 'perfick'. The drama gained a huge following among viewers who were weary of the prevailing trend for hard-bitten realism. It offered instead a sun-drenched, idyllic England and set the template for the Sunday-evening nostalgia slot later to be filled by *Heartbeat*.

The show was just one of many successes for David Jason, but it was a much more important landmark in the career of Catherine Zeta Jones. It gave her her first big break, and by the end of the decade she had become part of Hollywood royalty when she married Michael Douglas.

Permission to speak, sir
⇨ See **Dad's Army**

phone a friend
⇨ See **Who Wants to Be a Millionaire?**

146

play one's joker

It's a Knockout

The successful BBC series *It's a Knockout* aired from 1966 to 1982 and featured amateur teams from various British towns attired in ridiculous costumes competing in absurd quasi-athletic events. Commentary was provided by David Vine and Stuart Hall, whose irreverent hilarity was given a more down-to-earth counterpoint by genial but on occasions hard-to-follow rugby league commentator Eddie Waring.

The programme was one of the BBC's most popular shows in the 1970s, attracting up to 19 million viewers to watch teams get soaking wet and filthy dirty tackling a range of contests involving greasy poles, log-rolling, pillow fights, bungee runs and the like. Running through each episode was a 'mini marathon' which generally consisted of team members transporting water to a large measuring cylinder over some kind of obstacle course using an implausibly shaped receptacle while being pelted with soft objects by the opposition. An international European version of the game started in 1967 under the name *Jeux Sans Frontières* (the literal translation of which, 'Games Without Frontiers', provided Peter Gabriel with the title of a single that got to number 4 in the UK charts in February 1980).

The scoring system was relatively straightforward, with a twist added by the innovative 'joker' concept: if Lowestoft, Congleton or Market Harborough felt confident of winning a particular event, they could **play their joker**. This involved a member of the team coming up to the large manually operated scoreboard and parading an oversized playing card. If the team then won, their points for that game would be doubled. The phrase 'playing the joker' is still sometimes used to indicate that a certain thing has been identified as the target for maximum effort.

It's a Knockout was briefly revived in the 1990s, using the same format, but fronted by Keith Chegwin and Frank Bruno, who proved sadly unable to fill the shoes of their mighty predecessors.

plonker

Only Fools and Horses

David Jason's character of Del Boy Trotter in *Only Fools and Horses* (see page 142) is noted for his colourful put-downs and misguided use of foreign words. In a recent opinion poll, viewers were asked to nominate their favourite Del Boy catchphrase, and came up with no fewer than 18 different suggestions, including 'Mange-tout, mange-tout', 'He who dares, wins' and 'You tart!' However, there was no doubt about the winner, with 19 per cent of fans plumping for 'You **plonker**!'

The slang word 'plonker' has been around since the 1960s. It usually means 'a stupid person', although it can also be used to refer to the penis. The fact that the word is a relatively mild insult makes it suitable for family television, but the more risqué second meaning may have contributed to its appeal with audiences. It is interesting to note that Del Boy's most likely alternative insult, 'dipstick' (see page 42), carries the same dual meaning.

'Plonker' first featured in a script of *Only Fools and Horses* in the third episode, entitled 'Cash and Curry', and it soon became recognized and imitated. Indeed, it is so closely identified with the programme that saying 'You plonker!' prompts many Brits to complete the phrase with 'Rodney', alluding to Del Boy's long-suffering younger brother, who was usually the target of the insult.

> DEL: How can anything be too cheap, you plonker?
>
> MAN: Listen, I'm not a plonker!
>
> DEL: No? So what you doing? An impression?

Points make prizes

Play Your Cards Right

Bruce Forsyth is probably responsible for creating more television catchphrases than any other individual. Not content with coining several on *The Generation Game* (see page 184), Brucie thought up a stack more for the game show *Play Your Cards Right*, which ran on and off on ITV from 1980.

The format was based on the American programme *Card Sharks* and involved couples answering questions based on the results of opinion polls, such as 'In a survey of 100 marriage guidance counsellors, how many replied that they had been unfaithful to their partner?' The first couple would offer a figure, and the second couple would then judge in which direction this estimate erred. At this point, Brucie would intervene and canvass the audience with the question 'Higher or lower?' Whoever won this section was awarded points, prompting Forsyth to state that, '**Points make prizes**', quickly following up this assertion with the question 'What do points make?', to which the mob would reply deliriously, 'Prizes!'

The second section of the show involved a card game in which a row of cards was shown face down. The first card was turned over and one of the couples would guess whether the next card in the line was of a higher or lower value. Once again there would be much highering and lowering from the audience. If the next card was revealed to be of exactly the same value, Bruce wheeled out another catchphrase, '**You get nothing for a pair ...**', which the audience completed with the words, '**... not in this game**'.

The show also used some less successful catchphrases. Each edition would begin with, 'It's gonna be a good night tonight if you play your cards right', while commercial breaks were preceded with the warning, 'Don't touch the pack; we'll be right back.' Then there was Bruce's greeting to the glamorous female assistants who shuffled and dealt the cards, 'Here they are, they're so appealing; come on Dollies, do your dealing.' These 'Dolly Dealers' may well have put the feminist cause back a few years, but they did no harm to the ratings of *Play Your Cards Right*, which helped maintain Forsyth's reputation as one of television's most reliable performers.

Porridge

The British situation comedy *Porridge* was written by Dick Clement and Ian La Frenais and was broadcast between 1974 and 1977. Set in the fictional Slade Prison, it featured Ronnie Barker as the recidivist thief Norman Stanley Fletcher, Richard Beckinsale as his naive cellmate Lennie Godber, Fulton Mackay as the sadistic warder Mr Mackay, and Brian Wilde as his mild-mannered counterpart Mr Barrowclough. Other notable actors who appeared regularly on the show included David Jason, Christopher Biggins, Peter Vaughan and Ronald Lacey.

The programme started life as one of seven one-off pieces written by Clement and La Frenais to showcase Barker's comic talents, but eventually ran for three series and also spawned two Christmas specials, a full-length feature film and a spin-off called *Going Straight*, which chronicled Fletcher's adventures after his release and featured a young Nicholas Lyndhurst.

Porridge is notable for popularizing a number of items of slang, often indulging in euphemism in order to find a compromise between the kind of language appropriate to a family programme shown before the watershed and the sort of thing one might actually hear from people detained at Her Majesty's pleasure.

Perhaps the most flexible of these slang terms is the word '**naff**', which was used in the show as a mild swearword in a variety of different phrases, including '**naff all**' (nothing), '**naff off**' (an injunction to go away) and '**naffing**' (an all-purpose intensifier). In each case, 'naff' is used as a more socially acceptable form of the F-word. (It is perhaps worth noting that the use of 'naff' as an adjective referring to something that is embarrassingly unfashionable is unrelated to this word and probably comes from a dialect word for a fool or simpleton.)

With more colourful terms of abuse being off the table, the best that the inmates of Slade could manage was to call a despised person a '**nerk**' (see page 138) or a '**scrote**'. Both of these terms had existed before *Porridge* but became more popular in the 1970s as a result of the show's influence. In fact the words are spelt as 'nurk' and 'scroat' in the original scripts, playing down their derivation from 'berk' and 'scrotum' respectively.

Inmates might call someone a nerk or a scrote if they suspected they were trying to 'pull a **stroke**'. In the language of Slade prison, a 'stroke' means a dishonest or underhand act, the likes of which often propelled the drama in *Porridge* as individuals attempted to get one up on their fellow inmates or on the '**screws**' (as the prisoners called their warders). This latter term originated in the era when the locks on prison-cell doors were screwed shut. Besides being a standard term in *Porridge*, it is familiar to viewers from other prison-based TV series, such as *Bad Girls* and *Prisoner: Cell Block H*.

Another long-standing item of prison slang that became familiar through *Porridge* was '**snout**', referring to the tobacco or cigarettes that served as currency for transactions between inmates. This usage dates from the 19th century and is probably derived from the old practice of prisoners covering their 'snouts' (noses) with their hands to disguise the fact that they were smoking.

Power to the people!

Citizen Smith

The slogan '**Power to the people!**' was popularized by the Black Panther movement in America in the 1960s, and has been used to promote a range of populist causes. For many people in the UK, however, these words are indelibly associated with a gangling figure in an Afghan coat, black beret and Fulham scarf, raising a clenched fist towards the sky.

This was Wolfie Smith, hero of the BBC sitcom *Citizen Smith*. Wolfie (played by Robert Lindsay) was the brains behind the Tooting Popular Front, an organization making a largely futile attempt to champion radical politics in 1970s London. Over 30 episodes aired between 1977 and 1980, Wolfie adopted the posture of the urban guerrilla and mouthed revolutionary slogans picked up from the campuses of America, but his ambitions of establishing a socialist utopia in south London were constantly undercut by the mundane realities of coping with financial hardship and his girlfriend's disapproving father (played by Peter Vaughan). The viewers knew there was no chance that 'the glorious day' of the revolution would ever dawn.

Wolfie was fighting a losing battle in the late 1970s, and the appetite for a Marxist revolution has declined still further in the decades since *Citizen Smith* was screened. Nevertheless, his classic call to arms has been taken up in several other places. In 2003, for example, *The Economist* knowingly used 'Power to the people' as the headline for an article about the role of the Internet in promoting direct democracy. The slogan 'Power to the people!' has also been adopted by campaigners attempting to find a solution to California's energy crisis, for whom seizing the means of production is somewhat less of a concern than being able to keep the lights on.

pukka
The Naked Chef

When celebrity chef Jamie Oliver burst on to the television cookery scene in the late 1990s he was viewed as a breath of fresh air in a world dominated by middle-aged matriarchs. His show *The Naked Chef* ran for three series from 1999 to 2001 and led to two bestselling spin-off books. After a while, however, his increasing exposure sparked a backlash and a number of critics questioned the authenticity of his chirpy and cheerful Essex-boy persona. To use one of Oliver's own catchwords, there was some doubt as to whether Jamie was '**pukka**'.

'Pukka' is one of many words that English picked up from the Indian sub-continent. Derived from the Hindi word *pakka*, which means 'cooked', 'ripe' or 'substantial', it has been used in English since colonial times to mean 'genuine' or 'first-rate'. More recently, it was briefly adopted by British youths as an alternative to such slang terms of approval as 'ace' and 'wicked'.

It was in this sense that Oliver appropriated it in his show as part of a repertoire of hip slang that aimed to bring cookery to a new and younger audience. Yet before long, Oliver found that it had turned him into something of a joke. In his later programmes *Jamie's Kitchen* (2002) and *Jamie's School Dinners* (2005) he tried to limit his use of the word, telling the *London Evening Standard*, 'I've always said it but I try to avoid it now because I felt like I was becoming a cartoon of myself.'

Purdey cut

The New Avengers

No hairdressing salon could hope to stay in business for long in the mid-1970s if it could not offer its customers a **Purdey cut**. This look involved cutting the hair into a pageboy style with a deep fringe of the kind sported by Joanna Lumley in the action series *The New Avengers*, and it became de rigueur for young women of the period.

The New Avengers, which ran from 1976 to 1977, was a follow-up to the popular 1960s action series *The Avengers*. Like its forerunner, it was created by writer Brian Clemens and starred Patrick Macnee as the debonair British agent John Steed. In *The Avengers*, Macnee had received assistance from the likes of Honor Blackman and Diana Rigg. This time Gareth Hunt joined the team in the role of tough guy Mike Gambit, while ex-Bond-girl Lumley provided the glamour as agent Purdey, a former ballerina with dazzling looks, a sharp line in wit, a mastery of martial arts and an unlimited wardrobe budget. In fact, Purdey had pretty much everything – except a first name.

Indeed, even the one name that Purdey did possess was the subject of some debate. The original plan was to call the character 'Charley', but this had to be shelved to avoid confusion with a popular brand of perfume. It was apparently Joanna Lumley herself who came up with 'Purdey', naming the character after a prestigious make of shotgun.

Pythonesque

⇨ See **Monty Python's Flying Circus**

Rachel cut

⇨ See **Friends**

red zone
⇨ See **Snickometer®**

ridonkulous
⇨ See **The OC**

Say what you see
Catchphrase

The game show *Catchphrase*, which was first broadcast on ITV in 1986, is a bit of a misnomer. The contestants on this show are not asked to identify catchphrases, but to divine idiomatic phrases suggested by a pictorial clue that appears on a screen.

However, presenter Roy Walker did coin a popular catchphrase of his own during his spell as host, asking the contestants to '**Say what you see**' as they trained their eyes on the computer-animated clues featuring a yellow robot called Mr Chips. However wide of the mark the answers might be, Walker managed to remain patient and encouraging, greeting even the most ludicrously inappropriate guesses with the formula, 'It's good, but it's not right.'

Walker left the show in 2000 to be replaced by presenters Nick Weir and Mark Curry as the show slid from its peak-time weekend slot into the anonymity of a daytime berth on a satellite channel.

Scooby snack

⇨ See **... if it hadn't been for those pesky kids**

Scorchio!
The Fast Show

The exclamation '**Scorchio!**' is likely to be heard in the UK whenever the temperature nudges 70° Fahrenheit, and a heat wave is optimistically declared.

The word is a vaguely Hispanicized version of 'scorcher', the tabloid press's favourite designation for a very hot day, and was coined by *The Fast Show* (see page 183) as part of a regular sketch depicting a news programme broadcast by the fictional TV station 'Chanel 9'. The station was based in an unnamed country, but from the strange hybrid of Spanish, English and complete gobbledygook spoken, viewers could infer that it was under the control of a military dictator and that it was very, very hot. The joke lay in transferring the British obsession with the weather to a place where the weather never changed. Caroline Aherne's colourful but dizzy weathergirl Paula Fisch announced every day that it would be 'scorchio'. When, after so many days of unbroken sun, her usual bubbly manner was replaced by a demeanour of bored grumpiness, no-one was in any doubt what it meant.

Needless to say, the temperatures proclaimed in the forecasts of Ms Fisch (whose surname constitutes a nod to veteran British weatherman Michael Fish) were rather higher than might be expected on British shores. However, the sketch was so popular that 'Scorchio!' became a favourite catchphrase of the 1990s, even if it usually did require some stretch of the imagination.

scores on the doors
⇨ See **The Generation Game**

Scouse git
⇨ See **Alf Garnett**

screw
⇨ See **Porridge**

Screw you guys, I'm going home
⇨ See **South Park**

scrote
⇨ See **Porridge**

shilly-shally
Grandstand

Rugby union has, for many people, never been the same since Bill McLaren retired. Poetic flourishes are now largely absent from television commentaries. No longer are wingers 'flying machines' or prop forwards 'ample citizens'. 'Raging rhinoceroses' are few and far between and when a full-back scampers down the pitch evading a tackle with a neat sidestep, it is never described as 'a little **shilly-shally**'.

Bill McLaren, so far the only non-player to be inducted into Rugby Union's Hall of Fame, is a commentating legend. As a young man, he nearly died of tuberculosis, and it was while convalescing in hospital that he started commentating on table tennis matches for hospital radio. He found that he had a knack for it. By 1953 he was commentating on rugby for BBC radio. From there he moved to BBC television, where he was the voice of the sport for nearly five decades, commentating on games for *Grandstand* and *Rugby Special*.

Born and raised in the rolling hills of the Scottish Borders, McLaren often slipped agricultural metaphors into his commentaries. A huge number eight forward might be described as 'seventeen stones on the hoof' while a flanker breaking away from the scrum would 'charge like a Pamplona bull'. When players became ill-disciplined McLaren was often at his best, euphemistically describing mass brawls as 'a wee bit of argy-bargy' and foul play as 'shenanigans' or 'jiggery-pokery'. Such delightful turns of phrase are sadly missed by armchair fans, as modern commentators increasingly describe the game in technical terms or with the jargon of the sports psychologist.

short fat hairy legs

The Morecambe and Wise Show

The comedians Eric Morecambe and Ernie Wise were quite simply the most successful double-act in the history of British television, earning themselves the status of national treasures through their long-running *The Morecambe and Wise Show* (see page 208).

Their routine took on its familiar shape during their first ITV series, broadcast live each week from the Wood Green Empire in north London between 1961 and 1968. Regular gags included funny-man Eric grabbing straight-man Ernie by the throat and yelling 'Get out of that!' and making constant reference to Ernie's '**short fat hairy legs**' and the fact that, even though Ernie supposedly wore a wig, you 'couldn't see the join'. The reference to Ernie's undersized and hirsute lower limbs has since passed into the English language as a description of affectionate ridicule.

The phrase was even used as a source of comic by-play when The Beatles guested on *The Morecambe and Wise Show* in April 1964. Paul McCartney greeted Eric Morecambe with the line, 'I remember you. You're the one with the short fat hairy legs!' When Morecambe pointed out that it was his partner who had the short fat hairy legs, George Harrison chipped in with, 'We're the ones with the big fat hairy heads. Get out of that!'

Shut that door!

Shut That Door!

Larry Grayson's exaggerated camp persona made him an easy target for impressionists. Yet in 1979 even he must have been surprised to see the members of Abba attempting to imitate him. The Swedish superstars were guests on *Mike Yarwood's Christmas Special* that year. They appeared in a pastiche of *The Generation Game* and there was much hilarity as the Scandinavian quartet attempted to take off some of Grayson's best-known catchphrases, with Frida's '**Shut that door!**' being particularly well received.

Grayson had taken over *The Generation Game* from Bruce Forsyth in 1978. Under his tenure the format of the show stayed the same, but his trademark 'Shut that door!' catchphrase was worked into the theme song. This was just one of a number of phrases associated with the comedian who started life as William White, and then worked on stage as Billy Breen, before finally achieving success as Larry Grayson. He had started working in show business as a child, but it took him many years of performing as a drag act before he hit the big time with a guest spot on *Saturday Variety* in 1971. This was so successful that he was given his own show called *Shut That Door!* on ITV the following year. It was here that the public became familiar with catchphrases such as 'What a gay day!', 'Seems like a nice boy', and 'Look at the muck in here!' His stand-up act, which was naughty but never vulgar, also made use of monologues where he would mention his fictional friends Slack Alice, Everard, Apricot Lil and the postman, Pop-it-in Pete.

His best-known catchphrase is said to have its origins in the days before his TV career, when he would perform at venues where the privacy of the guest turns was not given high priority. He and his agent constantly found themselves asking departing visitors to the dressing room to 'Shut that door!'

SIG

Captain Scarlet and the Mysterons

'**SIG**' was the sign-off phrase used by members of the group Spectrum during their battles with the Mysterons (see page 134) as part of the puppet series *Captain Scarlet and the Mysterons*. Spectrum, which was based in an airborne headquarters called Cloudbase, was a colourful organization in more than one sense.

Firstly, every male member of Spectrum was given a colour code name – Captain Scarlet, Captain Blue, Colonel White, Captain Grey, Lieutenant Green, Captain Ochre, Captain Magenta, Doctor Fawn and Captain Black, the one who went over to the dark side (with a name like that he just had to be the bad guy). How many of these are colours of the spectrum – or even colours at all – is open to debate, but we don't want to get too hung up on physics here. (Spectrum also included five female members – jump-suited fighter pilots with big hair – who were collectively known as the Angels: Destiny, Rhapsody, Melody, Symphony and Harmony.)

Secondly, *Captain Scarlet* was notable for featuring Gerry Anderson's first black puppet character. He had wanted to include non-Caucasian characters for some time, but had earlier been persuaded that this might make it difficult to sell his material to the American market. However, the social climate had changed by 1967, and so Trinidadian Lieutenant Green and Tokyo-born aviatrix Harmony Angel were duly introduced.

Finally, there was the 'SIG' sign-off which served as the equivalent of the thumbs-up or of *Thunderbirds*' 'FAB' (see page 199). But unlike 'FAB', 'SIG' actually meant something, standing for 'Spectrum is green.' Apart from being demonstrably untrue – you don't have to be a physicist to know that the electromagnetic spectrum contains a much broader range of colours – 'SIG' is a pretty cool catchphrase and soon caught on.

silly old moo

⇥ See **Alf Garnett**

Sir Humphrey

Yes, Minister

For many years a word of Chinese origin, 'mandarin', was a favoured term for a high-ranking civil servant. More recently, such characters have come to be called '**Sir Humphreys**', a name that comes from a TV show much closer to home.

Sir Humphrey Appleby was – or thought he was – the man in charge of the Ministry for Administrative Affairs. As Permanent Secretary to the Ministry he theoretically had to take orders from the government Minister, James Hacker, but Sir Humphrey knew where the real power lay. Before he started his job as Minister, Hacker thought that politics was a straightforward business where common sense prevailed and civil servants carried out ministers' orders without question. Sir Humphrey soon disabused Hacker of this rather quaint notion, attempting to foil the Minister's boat-rocking initiatives at every turn. Therein lay the rich comic appeal of *Yes, Minister*.

Yes, Minister, written by Antony Jay and Jonathan Lynn, is one of Britain's most highly acclaimed sitcoms. From 1980 to 1988, it charted the political career of James Hacker (Paul Eddington), who started off in one of the government's least important ministries but ended up in Number 10, a move which prompted the show to change its name in 1986 to *Yes, Prime Minister*.

Most episodes featured a set-piece showdown where Sir Humphrey (Nigel Hawthorne) would bamboozle Hacker with a lengthy passage of officialese, such as the following speech from the 1981 episode 'The Death List': 'Well it was a conversation to the effect that, in view of the somewhat nebulous and inexplicit nature of your remit, and the arguably marginal and peripheral nature of your influence on the central deliberations and decisions within the political process, there could be a case for restructuring their action priorities in such a way as to eliminate your liquidation from their immediate agenda.'

Such bravura passages were just one feature of a sitcom that always had intricate plots, razor-sharp scripts and top-quality acting. Millions loved *Yes, Minister* and it even got the seal of approval from Downing Street. Margaret Thatcher, the serving Prime Minister, was a huge fan and even penned a short sketch based on the show, which she performed with members of the cast.

sixty-four-thousand-dollar question

The 64,000 Dollar Question

How can we solve the problem of third-world poverty? What makes a man attractive to women? How can you stop fluff accumulating in your navel? All of these conundrums, which seem to be of crucial importance but do not have an obvious answer, have been described at one time or another as the '**sixty-four-thousand-dollar question**'.

The expression comes from an American game show that started life on the radio in the 1940s but moved to television in 1955. The radio show was called *The 64 Dollar Question*, but what with inflation and with everything being on a bigger scale on television, the name was changed to *The 64,000 Dollar Question* for the small screen.

The show was hosted by Hal March and involved contestants answering a series of questions on a subject of their own choosing, each question being more difficult than the one before. As long as the contestant answered correctly, the cash prize on offer would be doubled, up to a maximum of $64,000. A contestant who could answer the sixty-four-thousand-dollar question correctly got to go home with the money.

In 1956 a British version called *The 64,000 Question* was launched, hosted by Jerry Desmonde and offering a top prize of 64,000 sixpences (£1,600). However, Harold Macmillan used the original American version of the phrase in his famous 'Never had it so good' speech of July 1957, which probably contributed to that form of words becoming established on both sides of the Atlantic.

smeg

Red Dwarf

If you think that the term '**smeg**' sounds a bit disgusting, your intuitions are entirely correct. This eminently flexible swearword – it is used in all sorts of functions and combinations, including '**smeg off**', '**smegging**', '**smeggy**' and '**smeghead**' – was devised by writers Rob Grant and Doug Naylor for the cult BBC science-fiction comedy series *Red Dwarf*, which began life in 1988 and has run for eight series. As with 'naff' in *Porridge* (see page 150) and 'feck' in *Father Ted* (see page 61), 'smeg' allowed the characters to curse without using conventionally taboo words. Also like those words, it was soon adopted with gusto by fans.

The ultimate origin of 'smeg' lies in the word 'smegma', which is – innocently enough – a Greek word for 'soap'. However, this is not the whole story: this term is generally used to refer to what the dictionary coyly calls 'a sebaceous secretion', more specifically one found under the foreskin of the male member. Smegma occurs in uncircumcised individuals with poor levels of personal hygiene, and decency forbids the divulging of further information.

This level of foulness is wholly appropriate to the character who uses the word most liberally in *Red Dwarf* – the incorrigibly laddish Dave Lister (played by Craig Charles). Lister emerges from three million years of suspended animation to discover the entire human crew of the spaceship *Red Dwarf* has been wiped out by a radiation leak. He does, however, have some non-human company on his adventures in space: Arnold Rimmer (Chris Barrie), a holographic reproduction of the incompetent original responsible for the catastrophe; Cat (Danny John-Jules), a highly evolved and very groovy feline; Holly (played variously by Norman Lovett and Hattie Hayridge), the ship's laconic computer and a spoof of HAL in *2001: A Space Odyssey*; and Kryten (played by David Ross and later Robert Llewellyn), a fussy robotic servant resembling C3PO in *Star Wars*.

Incidentally, the name *Red Dwarf* is a bit of a joke: astronomically speaking, there is a class of celestial body known as a white dwarf, and there is one known as a red giant, but there is no red dwarf. Or white giant, for that matter.

Smile, you're on Candid Camera

Candid Camera

Smiling was probably the last thing that anyone would feel like doing if, after being caught up in an inexplicable or embarrassing situation, they heard the phrase '**Smile, you're on Candid Camera.**'

Candid Camera was originally an American TV show which first aired in 1948, the brainchild of Allen Funt, and a form of the show is still being made in the United States. The British version appeared in 1960 and, presented by Bob Monkhouse, ran until 1967. It was briefly revived in 1974, when it was presented by Peter Dulay, but failed to repeat its earlier success.

The basic premise of the show was to involve unsuspecting members of the public in sustained practical jokes carried out by a team of actors (such as Jonathan Routh in the British version), and to film their reactions unseen. A lot of the humour came from people's attempts to deal sensibly with a ludicrous set-up, such as the classic example when a car was pushed into a garage forecourt for repair and the mechanic was dumbfounded to discover that it had no engine.

Most people took it in good part when they were finally told what was going on, but the occasional actor ended up with a black eye. The team was also reported to the police for behaving suspiciously in the vicinity of a bank and was almost arrested. Legend has it that, after this, local police forces had to be informed whenever the programme was filming.

The concept of this type of stunt was later taken up by other TV practical jokers such as Jeremy Beadle, Noel Edmonds and Dom Joly, but they, of course, did not use the famous catchphrase.

Snickometer®
Channel 4 Cricket

In 1999 Channel 4 won the rights to cover cricket on British terrestrial television. Armed with a brief to extend interest in the sport beyond its traditional followers, the commercial channel employed all manner of high-tech devices to enhance viewers' enjoyment and understanding of the game. One such device was the **Snickometer®**, a gizmo consisting of a microphone placed near the stumps which picks up sounds and records them on a graph. When used in conjunction with cameras, the Snickometer® can help determine if the sound that inspired an appeal against the batsman was generated by the ball hitting the edge of the bat or if it was caused by an incidental collision of bat and pad or ball and pad.

Another innovation was **Hawk-Eye®**, named after its creator Dr Paul Hawkins. Consisting of a computer linked to six cameras at various points around the ground, this device is able to create a 3-D virtual-reality representation of every ball bowled. When a bowler appeals for leg before wicket, Hawk-Eye® can show whether the ball would have hit the stumps if the batsman had not got his legs in the way of it. The ability of pundits to explain cricket's arcane lbw law is further enhanced by the '**red zone**', a rectangular block superimposed, for the benefit of viewers, over the area of the pitch in line with both sets of stumps. Analysis of whether or not an appeal is justified often depends on whether the ball is shown to have pitched in this area.

Such technological wizardry has taken the game into a new age, but continuity with the past has been maintained by the presence in the commentary box of cricketing institutions Richie Benaud and Geoffrey Boycott. Benaud's commentating philosophy is that less is more, while Boycott's volume of words almost matches the volume of runs he compiled in his days as a dour but prolific opening batsman. As a commentator, Geoffrey is largely responsible for popularizing the term '**corridor of uncertainty**' – the area on and just outside the line of off stump where a batsman, not knowing whether to play or leave, does not like the ball to be bowled. Most cricket lovers would agree that this is an unusually poetic turn of phrase to have been championed by the normally blunt Yorkshireman.

snout

⮑ See **Porridge**

so

Friends

The idiosyncratic use of the word '**so**' probably ranks a close second to that of 'like' (see page 93) among the more remarkable changes to spoken British English brought about during the 1990s by imported TV programmes such as *Friends* (see page 54).

Before *Friends*, this adverb was often used between the verb 'to be' and an adjective, serving to intensify the force of the latter ('I am so tired', 'She is so clever', 'You're so vain'). After the show became popular, however, young people in Britain began to imitate its characters and use 'so' as an intensifier in grammatical positions where it had not previously been found. One such place was between an auxiliary verb and a participle in a verb phrase ('I am so going to kill you', 'I had so forgotten about it'); another was between the verb 'to be' and a complementary phrase, especially one in the negative ('That is so not my problem', 'He is so not worth bothering about').

The scripts of *Friends* supply numerous examples of this sort of thing: disenchanted with busking, Phoebe says, 'This whole like playing-for-money thing is so not good for me'; Rachel breaks up with Ross by telling him, 'We are so over'; and when Joey takes revenge on Chandler for hiding his underwear by putting on every item in Chandler's wardrobe, his flatmate remarks, 'That is so not the opposite of taking somebody's underwear!'

Showbiz lore attributes the origin of this use of 'so' to the American comic actress Roseanne Barr. When a member of the crew on her programme *Roseanne* crossed her, she is said to have come out with the phrase, 'You are so fired!' Perhaps this was merely a garbled expression that emerged spontaneously in a moment of anger, but the unorthodox syntax seems to have struck a chord and started a significant linguistic trend.

Sock it to me!

Rowan and Martin's Laugh-In

The phrase '**Sock it to me!**', although popularized by television, originally came from a line in Aretha Franklin's version of the song 'Respect'. Aretha added this line as a background vocal when she covered this Otis Redding song in February 1967, and it quickly reached a wider public when it was adopted as a catchphrase on *Rowan and Martin's Laugh-In*.

The *Laugh-In* was a fast-paced American sketch show starring Dan Rowan and Dick Martin. It started life as a one-off broadcast in September 1967, but proved so popular that it returned as a weekly show, broadcast from 'beautiful downtown Burbank' between January 1968 and May 1973. The show was notable for two things: a wall with windows through which members of the cast (which included at various times Goldie Hawn and Lily Tomlin) would appear and tell jokes, and its use of a number of classic catchphrases, including 'Here come de judge', 'Verrry interesting', 'You bet your bippy' and, most famously of all, 'Sock it to me!' This last line was regularly delivered by English-born actress Judy Carne as the precursor to her being subjected to some form of slapstick, such as being doused in water or catapulted through a trapdoor.

The importance of the *Laugh-In* in American cultural life of the period can be gauged from the fact that Richard Nixon took the opportunity to appear on the show during the 1968 presidential campaign, and delighted viewers simply by saying 'Sock it to me!' on air. Nixon's opponent, Hubert Humphrey, was also invited to appear, but he declined the invitation. Needless to say, it was Nixon who won the election.

softly softly

Softly Softly

The BBC series *Softly Softly* introduced one of British TV's first police good cop/bad cop double acts, the no-nonsense Charlie Barlow (Stratford Johns), an officer not averse to pounding interviewees into submission, and his sidekick the gentler John Watt (Frank Windsor). The two had initially been paired in the series *Z Cars* and the partnership proved so successful that in 1966 they were seconded to the Regional Crime Squad by the BBC for *Softly Softly*, which ran for ten years (although the title later changed to *Softly Softly – Task Force* after Barlow received a further promotion and then left to go it alone in the less successful *Barlow at Large*).

Z Cars had been set in the north of England in Newtown, but for *Softly Softly* Barlow and Watt headed down to the fictional Wyvern (supposedly near Bristol), where they took up their new posts of Detective Chief Superintendent and Detective Chief Inspector. Promotion did little to mellow DCS Barlow, who remained as tough, relentless and sharp-tongued as ever.

The show's title was initially borrowed by television from the motto of the Lancashire Constabulary Training School, and the term '**softly softly**' is now used to refer an entire philosophy of policing, and more widely to any form of problem-solving by patience and perseverance, as in 'a softly softly approach'.

This seems at odds with the abrasive, confrontational Britcop routine that first brought it to national attention. However, the apparent contradiction between being nice and getting one's way is resolved in the full form of the phrase – 'softly, softly, catchee monkey', an Ashanti proverb. It was quoted by Robert Baden-Powell (who later founded the Scouting movement) during his tour of West Africa in 1895–6: 'A smile and a stick will carry you through any difficulty in the world, more especially if you act upon the old West Coast motto, "Softly, softly, catchee monkey"'.

sonic screwdriver

⇨ See **Doctor Who**

169

South Park

No comedy has been so loved and loathed as *South Park*, yet it had humble beginnings, starting life as an animated Christmas card which only industry insiders got to see. This short film, *The Spirit of Christmas*, was crudely animated and featured near-the-knuckle humour. Many thought its animators, Trey Parker and Matt Stone, to be talented but probably unlikely to get their ideas fully realized. The doubters were wrong, however, and TV network Comedy Central backed the duo to make a full series, which went on to be a smash hit in the United States and around the world. As well as half-hour shows, Parker and Stone have animated, written and voiced a successful *South Park* feature film and even been nominated for an Oscar for one of the film's songs, 'Blame Canada'. They have also turned their hands to puppetry, creating a *Thunderbirds*-style action film *Team America: World Police* which satirized both ends of the US political spectrum as well as poking fun at North Korea's communist dictator Kim Jong-il.

South Park concerns the adventures of four eight-year-old boys living in a permanently snow-bound town in Colorado. Kyle (the Jewish one), Kenny (the incoherent one), Eric (the foul-mouthed fat one), and Stan (the unremarkable one) attend school and live with their parents just like normal kids. Their lives, however, are far from ordinary. The freedom that animation gives the series means that just about anything can happen and just about anyone can appear at any time. Zombies, aliens, Osama bin Laden and a giant mechanized Barbra Streisand have all appeared in a show in which nothing is taboo and no institution, subject, event or person is off limits as a subject of rude, crude and very funny humour.

The show has produced a number of popular and much imitated catchphrases, two of the best-known relating to the objectionable Eric Cartman. Cartman's mum spoils him terribly and he hates being made fun of or not being the centre of attention. When teased about his weight, he is apt to reply, '**I'm not fat, I'm big-boned**', and if he doesn't get his own way he storms off and shouts, '**Screw you guys, I'm going home**.'

Unlike the cosseted Cartman, Kenny McCormick comes from the wrong side of the tracks and his parents resemble the white-trash couples who can be seen squabbling on *The Jerry Springer Show*. He is the most mischievous of the four friends and is respected because of his greater knowledge of the adult worlds of sex and swearing. One remarkable thing about Kenny is that the audience can't understand a word he is saying because his face is always muffled by the hood of his coat. Even more remarkable is the fact that he is killed in every episode, usually in extremely violent circumstances, but always comes back to life in the next as if nothing had happened. When Kenny's demise occurs, one of his friends blurts out, '**Oh my God, they killed Kenny!**', to which another adds, 'You bastards!'

A rather strange legacy of the show is a term which is now sometimes used to describe a rambling, illogical and inconsequential legal argument: the **Chewbacca defence**. This derives from an episode where the South Park school's chef (voiced by legendary soul singer Isaac Hayes) sues a record company for stealing his material. The record company is defended by OJ Simpson's lawyer Johnnie Cochran, who ignores the issues at stake and bamboozles the jury with a nonsensical piece of sophistry about a *Star Wars* character called Chewbacca. The gist of this argument is that Chewbacca, a giant furry beast, couldn't possibly live on the planet of Endor as it is inhabited by much smaller creatures. He finishes his bizarre speech with the following summing-up: 'If Chewbacca lives on Endor, you must acquit! The defence rests.'

spitting image

Spitting Image

The expression '**spitting image**' is an adaptation of 'spitten image', which is itself a dialect form of the phrase 'spit and image'. In this phrase 'spit' means 'a close likeness', a sense that arises from the phrase 'as like him as if he had spit him out his mouth'.

All of these expressions for a person who appears to be identical to another date from a time well before the advent of television, but in the 1980s the expression 'spitting image' gained a new lease of life and came to be associated with imitations that could not conceivably have been confused with their originals.

The satirical show *Spitting Image* was created by the cartoonists Peter Fluck and Roger Law and ran from 1984 to 1996. Fluck and Law employed outlandish latex puppets to caricature leading figures from the world of politics and entertainment in a show that spared few members of the establishment from its withering satire.

Such was the impact of the show at its peak that for many viewers the *Spitting Image* versions of prominent figures became more real than the people themselves. David Steel never regained his credibility after being portrayed as a tiny boy in David Owen's pocket, while John Major had a hard time shaking off his characterization as a monochrome grey figure who only ate peas.

In a few cases, however, the show's targets welcomed the attention, believing it was a sign that they had truly arrived. Defence Secretary Michael Heseltine even tried to buy his *Spitting Image* puppet from the show's makers – without success.

starter for ten

University Challenge

In 1975, a team of Manchester University students achieved infamy on the highbrow TV quiz *University Challenge*. Protesting about the show's supposed bias towards their counterparts at Oxford and Cambridge, the bolshie students answered either 'Trotsky' or 'Lenin' every time quizmaster Bamber Gascoigne posed a '**starter for ten**'.

University Challenge first aired on Granada TV in 1962, and was hosted by Bamber Gascoigne until it was axed in 1987. The quiz was revived by BBC2 in 1994, since when it has been hosted by Jeremy Paxman. The show has a simple format in which two teams of four students compete to answer questions that test their general knowledge, with special emphasis on science, history and culture. Each round begins with a 'starter' question worth ten points, with the first contestant to press the buzzer getting to answer. Once a starter is answered correctly, the team is allowed to confer over three bonus questions worth five points each, usually on a related theme or topic.

Since its return, *University Challenge* has disproved the theory that revivals are always inferior to the original programmes. Jeremy Paxman's no-nonsense style and regular sets of questions on pop-culture subjects have kept audiences entertained and sustained the ratings. There have even been a number of spin-offs: in 2002, past winners of the quiz appeared on *University Challenge Reunited*; and the following year saw the launch of *University Challenge: The Professionals* in which teams from various industries and professions lock horns.

The show's 'starter for ten' catchphrase can be used facetiously whenever a tricky question is being posed. *Starter for Ten* was also used by David Nicholls as the title of a novel concerning the experiences of a first-year undergraduate, culminating in a disastrous appearance on *University Challenge*.

Star Trek

The most popular science-fiction television programme of all time, *Star Trek* was created in 1966 by Gene Roddenberry. Roddenberry had been a bomber pilot in World War II, and later worked as a commercial pilot and LA policeman. He wrote scripts for many TV shows before creating the series that would bring him enduring fame.

The original *Star Trek* ran for three years and 79 episodes, chronicling the voyages of the Starship *Enterprise* under the leadership of Captain James T Kirk (William Shatner). Roddenberry was also behind a sequel, *Star Trek: The Next Generation*, which ran from 1987 to 1994, but after his death in 1991 it was left to others to carry on his work in the later spin-offs *Deep Space Nine* (1993–9), *Voyager* (1995–2001) and *Enterprise* (2001–5).

A capsule of Roddenberry's ashes was sent into space to orbit the Earth for six years before burning up in the Earth's atmosphere. There is also an asteroid named after him, as well as a crater on Mars – all of which goes to show that *Star Trek* has become more than just a television programme. It has crossed the boundaries of its fictional universe and had a profound influence on the real world. Most science-fiction programmes and films owe it a more or less explicit debt; NASA regularly refers to the programme – the first space shuttle was called *Enterprise* – and acknowledges its role in heightening public interest in space exploration; and a 1993 study by Purdue University, Indiana, even found that *Star Trek* was the main source for American children's knowledge about science.

Star Trek has spawned a host of phrases that have become part of the English language, most notably '**Beam me up, Scotty**' (see page 13), '**It's life, Jim, but not as we know it**' (see page 80), '**Make it so**' (see page 125) and '**to boldly go**' (see page 203). Many programmes generate catchphrases, of course, but few can claim to have created a whole new language. Yet fans of *Star Trek* (popularly known as '**Trekkies**', although they themselves prefer to be called 'Trekkers') can be found at conventions consulting dictionaries of **Klingon** and conversing in its guttural tones. This language has been painstakingly compiled to represent the tongue of the *Enterprise*'s most persistent foe.

A *Star Trek* glossary

As well as providing some much-imitated phrases, *Star Trek* also coined a whole range of terms to describe the artefacts of the 23rd and 24th centuries ...

dilithium crystals	*a rare mineral used in a starship's warp drive*
holodeck (or holosuite)	*an area in which three-dimensional simulations are created so that crew members can act out scenarios*
phaser	*a hand-held weapon that can incapacitate or kill an opponent*
photon torpedo	*a powerful weapon consisting of matter and antimatter contained in a capsule that is fired faster than the speed of light*
replicator	*a device that can create instantly any object requested*
tractor beam	*a strong targeted force field used by a starship to tow or draw in another ship or object*
tricorder	*a multi-purpose gizmo used by 'away teams' visiting alien planets, allowing them to scan and analyse the surrounding area*
turbolift	*a high-speed lift that transports crew members between the different decks of a starship*
warp drive	*a device that allows starships to move faster than the speed of light – a physical impossibility in our current understanding of space and time – by means of a matter/antimatter reaction*
warp factor	*a measure of how fast a starship is travelling using its warp drive, based on a scale with a ceiling of warp 10*

statto
Fantasy Football League

Football attracts three types of people: those who love to play the game; those who love to watch it; and those who love to pore over its statistics. This latter group is best personified by a semi-fictional character, **Statto**, whose name has now entered English as a word for a person with an obsessive interest in the facts and figures of a subject.

Statto is an exaggerated persona of betting expert and racing pundit Angus Loughran. The character first appeared on TV in 1994, acting as a stooge to David Baddiel and Frank Skinner on the comedy programme *Fantasy Football League*. The conceit of this show is that the hosts and audience are lounging around in a flat having a knockabout discussion of the beautiful game. Meanwhile Statto, dressed in pyjamas and dressing gown, politely sits in the corner dispensing facts and figures while acting as an Aunt Sally for Baddiel and Skinner's laddish humour.

Statto's name has come to be used in Britain as a synonym for 'wonk' or 'anorak', without the attendant implication of social ineptitude. Partick Thistle footballer Stephen Craigan was happy to confess to being 'a bit of a statto' on his club's website, while the word could have been made to describe Messrs Duckworth and Lewis, the British academics who worked out the complicated system used to adjust victory targets in limited-over cricket matches in the event of a rain delay.

sticky-back plastic
⇨ See **Blue Peter**

Stolly

➪ See **Bolly**

stramash

Scotsport

The Scottish dialect has some wonderfully descriptive words: 'clishmaclaver' (incessant chatter), 'fantoosh' (ostentatious) and 'hochmagandy' (illicit sex), for example. Another Caledonian coinage is '**stramash**', which is much loved by football commentators north of the border and means 'an uproar or brawl'. This word dates back several hundred years and is possibly derived from the word 'smash'. In the context of football, it typically refers to a messy period of broken play in which players from both sides battle furiously in a confined space to win the ball. The onomatopoeic 'stramash' seems to describe this type of energetic tussle perfectly.

The word is primarily associated with the commentator Arthur Montford who, for many years, introduced *Scotsport*, Britain's longest running sports programme. Montford, known as 'The Talking Sports Jacket' on account of his loud checked blazers, appeared on *Scotsport* from its debut edition in 1957 until his retirement in 1989. A favourite target of Scottish impressionists, his other catchphrases included 'Up go the heads', 'What a sensation!' and the rather too frequently employed 'Disaster for Scotland!'

stroke

⇨ See **Porridge**

Stupid boy

⇨ See **Dad's Army**

Suits you, sir!
The Fast Show

In certain circles, no salacious suggestion or risqué reference would be complete without the addition of '**Suits you, sir!**' (usually accompanied by a short, sharp and lewdly appreciative 'Ooh! Ooh!')

The phrase was given life by Ken and Kenneth, the gentlemen's tailors of *The Fast Show* (see page 183), played by Paul Whitehouse and Mark Williams. In one of the show's regular sketches, this apparently genteel duo would cultivate a comfortable and pleasant relationship with a customer, complimenting him on his looks, dynamism and the cut of his trousers, before getting their kicks by letting rip with the full force of their licentious imaginings involving the customer and his 'lady friend'.

The appearance of Hollywood heart-throb Johnny Depp as the duo's victim in the final *Fast Show* was a demonstration of what a force the 'Suits you, sir' phenomenon had become, not least when Depp joined in the 'Ooh! Ooh!'s with quite obvious relish.

In fact, the actual words uttered on the show by Ken and Kenneth were 'Suit you, sir!', but – rather as the Lone Ranger's cry of 'Hi-yo Silver' is popularly quoted as 'Hi-ho Silver' – the public has preferred an inaccurate but more natural-sounding version of the phrase. 'Suit you, sir!' has also become popular with sub-editors, and can often be found in headlines of stories about gentlemen's fashion.

swingometer

BBC Election Coverage

The year 2005 saw the golden anniversary of one of the BBC props department's most popular inventions. From its primitive beginnings in 1955 to its current 3-D incarnation, the **swingometer** has been used to reflect shifting electoral allegiances and has made unlikely stars of two of its operators.

The swingometer is essentially just a dial with a movable pointer that indicates the percentage swing in the popular vote from one party to another and allows pundits to predict how many parliamentary seats are likely to change hands as a result. It was first unveiled as a simple prototype by Peter Milne in 1955, and was developed into a slightly more elaborate device when wielded by David Butler during the BBC's coverage of the 1959 general election. By 1964 the device was in the capable hands of Canadian psephologist Robert McKenzie, who became a fixture of the BBC's election-night coverage until his death in 1981. Peter Snow then took the reins, overseeing the swingometer's transformation from something a *Blue Peter* presenter could knock up to a high-tech virtual-reality graphic.

The swingometer is a simple yet effective contraption and has outlasted any number of other explanatory devices, most notably *Newsnight*'s infamous Gulf War sandpit. The pit, in which Peter Snow would excitedly line up model tanks in a manner reminiscent of Michael Bentine in *Potty Time*, was decommissioned after the end of hostilities and is now on display at the Imperial War Museum.

Tardis

Doctor Who

Few devices dreamed up by the writers of science-fiction programmes have had such enduring appeal as the **Tardis**, the time-travel device introduced to viewers by the long-running series *Doctor Who* (see page 44).

The word 'Tardis' is explained – as all fans of *Doctor Who* know – as being an acronym, standing for 'Time And Relative Dimensions In Space'. All self-respecting Time Lords have one of these things to help them zip from one dimension to the next. Indeed, not only can a Tardis travel through time and space, but it can also disguise itself like a chameleon to fit in with its surroundings. For the hero of *Doctor Who*, however, this facility has been on the blink since 1963. Arriving on earth for the first time, the Tardis adopted the disguise of a British police telephone box. The disguise became stuck, the Doctor has never bothered to get it fixed, and the Tardis has looked like that ever since. This may have caused the Doctor the occasional operational difficulty, but it has saved a lot of work for the BBC props department, and it has certainly provided the show with an iconic image.

A Tardis has another special feature: although it may look small on the outside, it is large on the inside and can accommodate any number of time travellers. This intriguing detail has caught the public's imagination, and anything that is roomier or more spacious than it first appears can now be described as being 'Tardis-like'. In December 2003, for example, the motoring critic of *The Australian* felt obliged to allude to the Tardis in this description of the Toyota Prius: 'Styling leans heavily towards Europe and this is not a bad thing. It's handsome from any angle and the snub nose and short tail belie its Tardis-like interior.'

tattifilarious

⇨ See **marmalize**

That's all, folks!
The Bugs Bunny Show

The phrase '**That's all, folks!**' has become a popular way of expressing finality in a light-hearted but authoritative manner. It is widely associated with cartoon character Bugs Bunny, who used this as a trademark ending to the cartoons in which he starred, first in the cinema, and then on his own TV slot, *The Bugs Bunny Show*, which ran on ABC in the United States from 1960 to 1972. This show was one of the first animated shows on prime-time television, and featured the much-loved rabbit introducing a series of Warner Brothers' *Looney Tunes* and *Merrie Melodies* cartoons, with Bugs sharing the spotlight with the likes of Daffy Duck, Elmer Fudd, Roadrunner and Porky Pig.

In fact, it was the stammering Porky Pig who first used the phrase 'That's all, folks!' at the end of the 1937 cinema short *Rover's Rival*. Both Porky Pig and Bugs Bunny were animated by the prolific Tex Avery and Chuck Jones, pioneers of the art form, who consciously tried to move away from the more naturalistic style developed by the rival Disney studio, producing something much more manic and surreal.

The voices for both characters were provided by Mel Blanc, who joined Warner Brothers in 1936 and also voiced many of the studio's other cartoon characters, including Sylvester the cat, Foghorn Leghorn, Woody Woodpecker and Daffy Duck, becoming the first person to receive a screen credit for such work. He died in 1989 after a lifetime of bringing pleasure to millions, and his tombstone contains in large capital letters the words 'THAT'S ALL, FOLKS!'

That's you, that is

Newman and Baddiel in Pieces

In the early 1990s, comedians Rob Newman and David Baddiel were able to sell out huge venues for their live shows, leading to speculation that comedy was becoming 'the new rock'n'roll' – although there was some doubt as to whether the double act would emerge as its Lennon and McCartney or its Captain and Tennille.

Newman and Baddiel first made their names alongside Steve Punt and Hugh Dennis in the satirical show *The Mary Whitehouse Experience* before striking out on their own and being given their own series, *Newman and Baddiel in Pieces*, which was broadcast on BBC2 in 1993. The show involved a mixture of stand-up monologues and sketches based around recurring characters. Probably the most successful of the regular sketches was 'History Today', which portrayed a pair of elderly academics whose ostensibly learned televised debates would rapidly degenerate into the trading of infantile insults. The stock routine involved describing some unappealing object and saying, '**That's you, that is.**' This sequence reduced many of the nation's students to the verge of hysteria, prompting them to copy it by, for example, pointing at a rubbish bin and declaring, 'See that? That's your house, that is. That's where you live.'

> "You know like a pair of pants with some cack in it. That's you, that is"

In spite of the success of this catchphrase, there was no second series. Newman pursued a career as a novelist while Baddiel has remained a familiar face on television through his long-running partnership with Frank Skinner in programmes such as *Fantasy Football League* (see page 176) and *Baddiel and Skinner Unplanned*.

The Fast Show

The Fast Show, a comedy sketch show first broadcast in 1994, may have been responsible for generating more memorable catchphrases than any comparable show in British television history. Created by Charlie Higson and Paul Whitehouse, who both also took on many of the roles in the show, *The Fast Show* took its name from its short – sometimes almost perfunctory – sketches. These featured a host of regular characters whose behaviour was often bizarre, but which, nevertheless, was grounded in a familiar and sometimes poignant reality.

Many of the characters had their own signature phrases, from the insecure woman who demanded to know 'Does my bum look big in this?' even when giving birth, to Swiss Toni, a middle-aged car salesman who fancifully imagined that most activities in life, including selling cars, were 'like making love to a beautiful woman'. The characters and their quirks struck a chord with the viewing public, and soon their catchphrases could be heard being bandied around in all kinds of situations – all guaranteed to raise a laugh. Indeed, this was so much the case that the show even made reference to it in the character of Colin Hunt, the office joker/bore who irritates everyone by repeating catchphrases from TV comedies.

The show ran for three series before finally bidding its audience farewell in 2000 with a three-part special in which the viewers' expectations of the characters, and their catchphrases, were turned upside down. But over its six-year run it had enlivened the way we talk with phrases such as '**I'll get me coat**' (see page 76), '**I was very, very drunk**' (see page 83), '**jumpers for goalposts**' (see page 86), '**Scorchio!** ' (see page 156), '**Suits you, sir!**' (see page 178), '**This week I have mostly been eating …**' (see page 198), '**Where's me washboard?**' (see page 209), '**… which was nice**' (see page 210) and '**With my reputation?**' (see page 215).

The Generation Game

The Netherlands enjoys a fairly high reputation in Britain as a country of culture and enlightenment. And this is in spite of the fact that it has exported both *Big Brother* and *The Generation Game* to our shores. In 1971, long before the reality TV behemoth *Big Brother* was plundered from across the North Sea, the BBC launched a new Saturday-night game show, basing it on the Dutch programme *Een Van De Acht* ('One From Eight'). Dancer, singer and comedian Bruce Forsyth was the host and he quickly established *The Generation Game* as appointment viewing.

The show's distinctive format used teams composed of two people from different generations of the same family (father and daughter, mother and son-in-law, and so on). The teams competed against each other in a series of trials. Typically these involved an expert, such as a master skilled in the Japanese art of ornamental vegetable carving, who would use a lifetime of skill and experience to create something pleasing to the eye, before the contestants were given a brief time to recreate the finished article using the same materials or ingredients. Much hilarity would ensue from their clumsy attempts and from Brucie's disdainful comments. Similar opportunities for embarrassment were afforded by subsequent challenges, which might involve the contestants attempting to emulate marching bands or Scottish country dancers. The trials were judged by the experts and points awarded for skill and style.

Once the contests had been completed, the ultimate winners of the show would then be given the chance to win some consumer durables. One member of the family would sit in front of a conveyor belt along which fabulous prizes (fabulous by the standards of the 1970s, that is) would be carried. Afterwards the contestant had to remember as many of the items as possible and shout them out while the clock counted down. A cuddly toy always featured among the procession of sandwich makers, bathrobes and fondue sets, and this would earn a small cheer of recognition from the audience.

Viewers' enjoyment of the show was enhanced by a string of catchphrases that Forsyth deployed at regular points each week. Although these were coined more than thirty years ago, many of them are still very familiar and are trotted out whenever the opportunity allows, such as when showing off a new item of clothing or expressing admiration at a plucky performance.

Each edition would open with Forsyth's greeting '**Nice to see you, to see you nice**', the last word of which was shouted by the studio audience. His female assistant, Anthea Redfern, was then introduced. Each week the future Mrs Forsyth would come onto the stage dressed in an eye-poppingly awful outfit which she would show proudly to the audience upon Bruce's command of '**Give us a twirl**'. Once Anthea had introduced us to the contestants, the games would commence. During these contests, Forsyth took every opportunity to get a laugh out of the ineptitude of the plucky competitors, but their efforts were usually rewarded in the end with '**good game, good game**' and '**Didn't she do well?**'

After hosting the show from 1971 to 1978, Bruce Forsyth left for ITV and Larry Grayson (see page 160) took over. Brucie returned for a second spell in the 1990s before Jim Davidson took the reins for the show's final run, which ended in 2002.

It was during Larry Grayson's tenure that another catchphrase was introduced. Bruce Forsyth had kept track of the contestants' running totals with the phrase '**Let's have a look at the old scoreboard**'. This catchphrase was ditched by his successor, who would instead ask the new hostess Isla St Clair, 'What are the **scores on the doors?**' (the scores for the two teams being displayed on the doors of cubicles that each team had to enter while the other was competing). Vic Reeves and Bob Mortimer later adapted Grayson's catchphrase on *Shooting Stars*, asking that show's recorder of points, 'What are the scores, George Dawes?' Later still, the surrealist duo went a step further, parodying the whole *Generation Game* format with their own game show *Families at War*.

The OC

First broadcast in 2004, *The OC* offered a formula of good-looking actors exchanging sharp dialogue and flaunting conspicuous wealth in sun-drenched locations. This was eagerly devoured by a generation of TV watchers attempting to come to terms with life after the recent demise of *Friends*, *Frasier* and *Sex and the City*.

The show's title is an abbreviation of Orange County, the prosperous area of southern California where the show's central characters live out their complicated lives against a backdrop of parties, yachts, swimming pools and fashion shows. At its heart is the wealthy but high-principled Cohen family, who take in Ryan Atwood (Benjamin McKenzie), a bright kid from the wrong side of tracks, in an attempt to save him from lapsing into a life of petty crime. After initial awkwardness, Ryan becomes best friends with the Cohens' self-conscious son Seth (Adam Brody), and the show chronicles the twists and turns of their teenage relationships with Marissa Cooper (Mischa Barton) and Summer Roberts (Rachel Bilson) respectively. However, the children are not the only ones with complicated lives: Marissa's parents in particular help to keep the plot turning with various financial and sexual shenanigans.

The show had a natural constituency in the teenage market, but it also had an ironic point of view and an intelligence that elevated it above the likes of *Beverley Hills 90210* and *Dawson's Creek* and gave it an appeal across a broader age-range. Above-average acting and a strong soundtrack did it no harm either.

While it is too soon to talk about the long-term impact of *The OC* on English, there have already been several claims that it has transformed the vocabulary of the younger generation.

While some elements of the Californian teen slang were already familiar from shows such as *Buffy the Vampire Slayer* (see page 26) and films such as *Bill and Ted's Excellent Adventure* (1989) and *Clueless* (1995), there was also plenty of linguistic novelty in the scripts. Josh Schwartz, the show's creator, peppered the dialogue with buzzwords and one-liners – often put into the mouth of his alter ego Seth – and many of these have been taken up with enthusiasm by the show's younger viewers. The show is widely credited with popularizing the term '**Chrismukkah**', referring to a combination of Christmas and Hanukkah celebrated by a family where one parent is Christian and the other Jewish (as is the case with the Cohens), and the relish with which the word 'yogalates' was treated helped to bring this brand of physical exercise to broader notice.

"Dude, I cannot believe you live in a penthouse, man. This place is ridonkulous!"

Another noteworthy item of vocabulary to have been popularized by the programme is the word '**ridonkulous**'. This humorous variation on the word 'ridiculous' is first recorded in the late 1990s, and is found in various spellings. In *The OC* it is a favourite adjective of Seth's and is used to indicate that something is so absurd that it almost defies belief.

The Simpsons

Created by Matt Groening, and starting off life as a brief interlude in an episode of *The Tracey Ullman Show* in 1987, *The Simpsons* became a full-length cartoon comedy series in 1989 on the Fox network in America. Following the adventures of the Simpson family – Homer (voiced by Dan Castellaneta), Marge (Julie Kavner), Bart (Nancy Cartwright), Lisa (Yeardley Smith) and Maggie (Matt Groening and, on one occasion, Elizabeth Taylor) – and their neighbours, friends, and colleagues in the town of Springfield, it has given TV some of its sharpest and funniest comedy and led the way for other adult-oriented animated shows such as *South Park* (see page 170) and *King of the Hill*.

As well as featuring a host of fictional characters, *The Simpsons* is well-known for enticing real-life stars to put in guest appearances, with famous people as diverse as Stephen Hawking and Tony Blair contributing their vocal talents. Obtaining the services of the British Prime Minister was a coup for the producers as they have so far been unable to lure a US President or ex-President onto the show. Although *The Simpsons* did get some publicity courtesy of President George Bush, Senior, of course: he famously said 'We need a nation more like the Waltons and less like the Simpsons' as part of a speech about family values. The remarks from the embattled President in fact did the show no harm, and the writers got their own back in a scene where the animated family was shown watching Bush's speech on television. Bart Simpson's reply to the unwarranted attack was, 'Hey, we *are* just like the Waltons: we're praying for an end to the depression too!'

The show is responsible for a number of catchphrases, two of the most notable ones being associated with the world's favourite tearaway, Bart Simpson. Whenever Bart is amused or surprised by something out of the ordinary he exclaims '**Ay caramba!**' Meaning 'gosh!' or 'wow!', this mock Latin-American interjection is perhaps inspired by the Brazilian samba tune 'Ay, Ay Caramba'.

A more controversial catchphrase of Bart's is the truculent '**Eat my shorts!**' A favourite with children of all ages, this has graced T-shirts, mugs, and other *Simpsons* merchandise, much to the outrage of killjoy parents and teachers.

Although Bart was originally viewed as the centrepiece of the show, his father Homer – described by Groening as being a dog trapped in a man's body – has emerged as a figure of even greater stature. Well-known for his clumsiness and failure to get things right first time, his characteristic cry of pain or exasperation is '**D'oh!**', and it can be heard at least once an episode. Dan Castellaneta, who provides the voice for Homer, apparently adapted the cry of 'Dooooooh' made by Scottish actor James Finlayson, the straight man in many of the Laurel and Hardy films of the 1920s and 1930s. This exclamation has become so familiar that it has been added to a number of English dictionaries.

The Sopranos

Cable channel HBO has defied the received wisdom that
Americans can't produce serious TV drama. Violent and
misogynistic it may be, but *The Sopranos* is also well written
and well acted, qualities that have gained it multiple Golden
Globe and Emmy awards. Moreover, since the first series was
broadcast in 1999, it has managed to treat mob life in New
Jersey with an original humour and style.

The show brings a special meaning to the term 'family drama',
examining the lead character Tony Soprano's relationships with
his wife, son, daughter, uncle, cousin and sister, as well as his
extended mob 'family'. But storylines weave in and out between
these families so much that it is sometimes hard for Tony
(played by James Gandolfini) to know if his 'family' is the mob
or his blood relatives. The euphemistic use of such everyday
words is rife in the programme (perhaps due to the characters'
fear of being overheard by the FBI): the mob life becomes
'this thing of ours' (the English translation of *cosa nostra*), and
killings are 'the thing' or simply 'it'. Similarly, a fellow mobster
is 'a friend of ours'. All of this is said in the distinctive New
Jersey accent where 't's become 'd's , vowels are flattened and
words are run together. This gives us two of the best-known
catchphrases of the show: '**Fuhgedaboudit**' (Forget about it),
a multi-purpose term of dismissal, and '**Wudayagonnado?**'
(What are you going to do?), expressing resignation.

The phenomenal popular and critical success of *The Sopranos*
has made millions more familiar with Italian-American

delicacies such as 'cannoli', 'braciole' and 'ziti' (a speciality of Tony's wife Carmela, played by Edie Falco), but has also introduced us to some colourful US gangster slang. While some of these terms remain as obscure to British viewers as the ingredients of cannoli (cream cheese in a pastry tube, since you ask), others – most notably the use of '**whack**' to mean 'murder' (see page 207) – are now creeping into the vocabulary of the British crime genre.

Gems of mobspeak with which *Sopranos* aficionados are now conversant include 'made guy' and 'wiseguy' (a mob member who has earned a certain status), 'consigliere' (a trusted advisor), 'capo' (a senior member in charge of a crew, also referred to as a 'captain'), 'goomah' (a mistress), 'shake down' (to extort money from someone) and 'stugots' (meaning testicles, from the Italian *stu cazzo*, and also the name of Tony's boat).

The Sopranos can also be credited with popularizing the expression '**Bada bing!**' – although the phrase, which means something like 'Hey presto!', predates the show. The Bada Bing (just 'the Bing' to its habitués) is also the name of the strip club owned by the Soprano family, a fictional version of a real-life New Jersey club called Satin Dolls. However, the programme makers boobed when they portrayed topless dancers on the show. They won't be seen on stage in Satin Dolls, as New Jersey state laws forbid topless dancing in bars where alcohol is served.

The Sweeney

Screeching through the mean streets of 1970s London in a mid-brown Ford Granada, Jack Regan and George Carter struck terror into the heart of every East-End gangster. In an era before political correctness, when women were 'birds' and smoking was compulsory, the Flying Squad's finest usually got the better of shooter-toting, balaclava-clad robbers, arresting them with a cry of 'You're nicked!' A tale of blags, slags, fags, and Jags, *The Sweeney* was (to use a phrase of Regan's) 'so hard you could roller-skate on it'.

The Sweeney first appeared in 1974, at a time when British police dramas were rather sedate. *Dixon of Dock Green* (see page 51) was at the end of its uneventful beat, while *Z Cars*, initially praised for its realism, seemed rather tame compared to its American rivals. Sensing a gap in the market, Ian Kennedy Martin wrote *Regan*, a pilot about a no-nonsense detective tackling serious crime. It was a success, and a series was commissioned for Thames Television. Renamed *The Sweeney* – Sweeney Todd, the legendary murderous barber, is rhyming slang for 'Flying Squad' – it ran between 1974 and 1978 and starred John Thaw and Dennis Waterman as Regan and Carter, two hard-drinking, chain-smoking womanizers with short tempers. Although both were basically honest coppers, they had no compunction about bending the rules to get the job done. Car chases were thrilling, and violent confrontations between police and criminals were depicted with bone-crunching realism. Occasional (female) nudity, (mild) swearing, and eminently hummable title music (penned by Harry South) also added to the show's appeal.

The Sweeney was a huge hit while it ran and has been repeated often since. It spawned two feature films and Waterman and Thaw even had the honour of appearing as guests on a Christmas edition of *The Morecambe and Wise Show*. The series has lingered long in the British imagination: in 1993 the Regan character was affectionately sent up by *The Comic Strip* in 'Detectives on the Verge of a Nervous Breakdown'; while in 1997, almost two decades after the show's final episode, a parody of *The Sweeney* was used to advertise the Nissan Almera.

A *Sweeney* glossary

In between punch-ups and shoot-outs, Regan and Carter peppered their dialogue with slang words from both sides of the law …

blag	*a crime*
blagger	*an armed robber*
dabs	*fingerprints*
governor	*a detective's boss*
helmet	*a uniformed police officer*
lids	*a collection of uniformed officers*
nark	*an informant*
nostrils	*a sawn-off shotgun*
plod	*a uniformed police officer*
shooter	*a gun*
slag	*a contemptible person*
snout	*an informant*
Sweeney	*The Flying Squad*
tooled up	*armed with weapons*
tom	*a prostitute*
woodentop	*a uniformed police officer*
You're nicked!	*I am arresting you*

The truth is out there

The X-Files

'**The truth is out there**' is not a conventional television catchphrase in that characters in *The X-Files* do not repeatedly say the words during the show. Instead, it appears as a tagline in the opening credits and neatly sums up the show's ethos. The facts, even if they are deliberately concealed or improbable, can be obtained through patient, independent inquiry.

The X-Files was created by Chris Carter and aired between 1993 and 2002. It concerned two FBI investigators who were given the task of looking into cases that seemed to defy rational explanation. Fox Mulder (David Duchovny) believes he witnessed his sister's abduction by aliens when they were children and is therefore predisposed to seek paranormal explanations for each case. Mulder's world view is summed up by the UFO poster bearing the legend 'I believe' which hangs in his office. His partner, Dana Scully (Gillian Anderson), is far more sceptical, at least initially. Over the course of the show, however, she becomes more willing to see the world through Mulder's eyes.

Government cover-ups and conspiracies loom large in *The X-Files*, and this was a big part of the show's attraction for its fanatical followers (known as 'X-Philes' or 'eXcers'). The show also had a sub-group of fans called 'shippers' (relationshippers), who charted the growing emotional bond between Mulder and Scully.

The show's main tagline has become firmly established in the collective consciousness. It is often used as a headline for a news story about UFOs or the paranormal. Stories where cover-ups and disinformation are alleged are also ideal candidates for an *X-Files* reference. In 2003, for example, *The Guardian* used it in a report about the Hutton inquiry into the events surrounding the death of government weapons specialist David Kelly.

Intriguingly, 'The truth is out there' is not the only tagline to feature in the opening credits of *The X-Files*. A number of one-off messages appear briefly on the screen at the start of some episodes. These include 'Trust no-one', 'Deny everything', 'All lies lead to the truth' and the ominous 'They're watching.'

The weekend starts here

Ready, Steady, Go!

'**The weekend starts here**' is often used as a Friday-night rallying cry urging people to forget the troubles of their working lives and relax. People have been pouring out of factories and offices on Friday evenings and cheering themselves with the thought since it was first adopted as a slogan by *Ready, Steady, Go!* in 1963.

Ready, Steady, Go! was broadcast on ITV live at six o'clock on Friday nights from a studio in London's Kingsway. The show consisted largely of pop groups – including the likes of The Beatles and The Rolling Stones – playing current hits and new releases in front of a studio audience, interspersed with occasional interviews. It was one of the first television programmes aimed specifically at the emerging teen market and was notable for featuring a teenage presenter, Cathy McGowan, who gave the programme a credibility with young people not shared by *Top of the Pops*, its nearest equivalent on the BBC. The show ended in 1966 at the height of its popularity, and is fondly remembered as one of the iconic programmes of the period.

Over thirty years later, its catchphrase was introduced to a whole new generation of young people when Fatboy Slim recorded a track called 'The Weekend Starts Here' on his 1997 album *Better Living Through Chemistry*.

the word on the street

Starsky and Hutch

Informants are a mainstay of TV cop shows, supplying their handlers with invaluable information when leads dry up or the trail goes cold. The malodorous Lonely (played by Russell Hunter) fulfilled this role for Edward Woodward's *Callan*, while *The Sweeney*'s Regan and Carter employed a variety of low-lifes prepared to grass up their fellow villains. In America, however, informants were a bit more glamorous. Huggy Bear, sporting a dazzlingly tasteless wardrobe, was aware of everything that happened on the wrong side of the tracks in the fictional Bay City, which was just as well for the eponymous heroes of *Starsky and Hutch*. In each episode of the iconic cop show, the two detectives would, after a period of head-scratching, approach Huggy for help with their case, asking the garishly dressed snitch for **'the word on the street'**.

Starsky and Hutch was an immensely popular American TV series which ran from 1975 to 1979. Starring Paul Michael Glaser as David Starsky and David Soul as Ken 'Hutch' Hutchinson, the show was a winning combination of crime fighting, male bonding and car chases. Added to that was a dash of 'blaxploitation', in the form of Antonio Fargas's Huggy Bear, and a memorably funky theme tune penned by Isaac Hayes. Even the heroes' car was a star in its own right, prompting dozens of British fans to paint their Cortinas red with a thick white stripe in homage to Starsky and Hutch's Ford Gran Torino.

The show's popularity endures. In 2004, a cinema version was filmed, starring Ben Stiller and Owen Wilson, with Glaser and Soul appearing in cameo roles. Although Antonio Fargas did not appear in the film, he turned up later in the year on the reality TV show *I'm a Celebrity, Get Me Out of Here!*, where he was known as 'Huggy' rather than Antonio, presumably for the benefit of more slow-witted viewers.

They don't like it up 'em

⇨ See **Dad's Army**

196

They think it's all over ...

BBC Sport

Live sports commentary is a tricky business. Slip-ups cannot be edited out, nor can ill-chosen words be left on the cutting room floor. The satirical magazine *Private Eye* is happy to repeat the howlers perpetrated by commentators in its 'Colemanballs' column, named after serial offender David Coleman.

Just as well, then, that the BBC's man on the spot found just the right words to go with the action at English football's finest moment. In the last minute of extra time in the 1966 World Cup final, England led West Germany 3-2. On one side of the ground, a number of fans thought they heard the referee's final whistle and began running onto the pitch to celebrate. Meanwhile, on the other side of the pitch, Geoff Hurst ran on to Bobby Moore's long pass and made his way toward the German goal. Ignoring the fans' invasion, he lashed a fierce shot into the roof of the net to make it 4-2 to England. Commentator Kenneth Wolstenholme managed to describe both the invasion and the clinching goal with the words, 'Some people are on the pitch ... **They think it's all over** ... It is now!'

As English successes have been few and far between since that triumph at Wembley, the 1966 World Cup final has become the most repeated piece of sporting action on British television. Rarely a month has gone by without a replay of Hurst's decisive goal, and Wolstenholme's words have taken their place in the nation's canon of patriotic quotations alongside 'We shall fight them on the beaches ...' and 'Once more unto the breach, dear friends, once more ...'

Wolstenholme's soundbite was iconic enough to be used as the title for a BBC comedy quiz in 1995. *They Think It's All Over*, introduced by Nick Hancock and featuring sporting stars such as Gary Lineker, David Gower, David Seaman and Phil Tufnell, provides a laddish alternative to the slightly more serious *A Question of Sport*. It also reminds us of the time England actually won the World Cup, just in case 1966 ever slips from our minds.

This is an ex-parrot
⇨ See **Monty Python's Flying Circus**

This tape will self-destruct in five seconds
⇨ See **mission impossible**

This week I have mostly been eating ...
The Fast Show

We all have our favourite foods, but not everyone feels the need to share their preferences with everyone else (especially when the food in question provides evidence of an imperfectly cultivated palate). However, for a time many people felt a new desire to share their dietary choices with a wider world, using the phrase '**This week I have mostly been eating ...**'

Behind this trend was 'Jesse's Diets', a regular sketch on *The Fast Show* (see page 183). This consisted simply of a shabbily dressed man called Jesse (played by Mark Williams) emerging from the shed that was his home to announce what had comprised the bulk of his diet for that week. Usually, this would be a foodstuff that would not exactly make the mouth water, such as bourbon biscuits or acorns. However, Jesse was not averse to surprising his audience with the likes of, 'This week I have mostly been ... bulimic.'

There was another surprise in the third series of *The Fast Show* when Jesse branched out into informing his public of his sartorial preferences ('This week I have mostly been wearing ... Dolce and Gabbana').

The element 'I have mostly been' is now frequently incorporated in accounts of people's lifestyles and routines. For example, one online diarist remarks that 'This year I have mostly been reading Heidegger', while a restaurant advertises itself with the words 'This week we have mostly been getting rave reviews in the *Sunday Times*.'

Thunderbirds are go!

Thunderbirds

Few programmes have such a memorable opening sequence as *Thunderbirds*. A countdown from five to one, with each number punctuated by a blare of brass, is followed by a rocket's blastoff before the words '**Thunderbirds are go!**' herald Barry Gray's stirring march played by a full orchestra.

Thunderbirds, a puppet series created by Gerry Anderson, has been enjoyed by children of all ages since 1965. The series, set a hundred years in the future, concerns the daring exploits of the Tracy family, a dynasty of astronauts and pilots whose Pacific island is the base for their emergency response team, International Rescue. Jeff Tracy is the head of the organization, while his sons John, Scott, Virgil and Gordon – all named after pioneering US astronauts – pilot powerful vehicles called Thunderbirds. Thunderbird 2 is the team's workhorse, having the capacity to be loaded with a variety of 'pods' each of which contains a different item of specialist equipment or a smaller vehicle.

The Tracy family can rely on assistance from the glamorous Lady Penelope, who is chauffeured by her faithful driver, Parker, in a pink Rolls Royce with the registration FAB1. The registration refers to the radio code '**FAB**', which members of International Rescue use to mean 'message received and understood'. Initially FAB was just a group of letters that sounded good but did not stand for anything, but many fans found this unsatisfactory. So Anderson eventually bowed to pressure and FAB was explained as an abbreviation of 'fully advised and briefed'.

Thunderbirds has been pastiched on a number of occasions. Soon after it was first shown, Peter Cook and Dudley Moore memorably lampooned the rather awkward and jerky movements of Gerry Anderson's puppets. Forty years later, in a tribute to the show's enduring appeal, the creators of *South Park* used *Thunderbirds*-style marionettes to great effect in the satirical feature film *Team America: World Police*.

tickling stick

⇨ See **marmalize**

Time for bed

The Magic Roundabout

The Magic Roundabout has provided two separate generations of
young children with a glimpse into a strange land where events are
controlled by a red, mustachioed jack-in-the-box-without-a-box
called Zebedee, who calls a halt to the dream-like, rather psychedelic
proceedings after the allotted five minutes with a magisterial '**Time
for bed.**' Nobody ever argues with him.

The programme was originally produced by Frenchman Serge Danot
in 1963 (with the French title *La Manège Enchantée*), but when it
was exported across the channel, British children got to see the same
surreal stop-frame animated characters but with entirely different
storylines, voiced firstly by Eric Thompson (father of Emma) in 1965,
and then by Nigel Planer (drippy hippy Neil from *The Young Ones*) in
1991 using 39 hitherto-unseen episodes.

Apparently, Eric Thompson decided to ignore the original scripts
altogether when doing his voice-over. Working with the volume
turned down, he rewrote the stories and redefined the characters,
injecting new wit and melancholy into the shows. Many critics
assumed the new storylines contained references to the 1960s
counterculture (the dog and his sugar cubes must refer to LSD, and
as for the rabbit, well, he was just toooo far out). So whereas French
children saw a dog called Pollux who spoke French with a comic
English accent, a Spanish-sounding rabbit called Flappy, a snail called
Ambroise and a little girl called Margote, in Grand Bretagne, the
dog was the dry, Hancock-like Dougal, the rabbit was the spaced-out
Dylan, the snail was cheery Brian and the girl was Florence.

The show's 'Time for bed' catchphrase is still used (often followed
by 'said Zebedee' to make the allusion clear), and in 1996 it even
provided comedian David Baddiel with title of his debut novel, a book
which concerns an insomniac suffering from unrequited love.

Time Lord

⇨ See **Doctor Who**

Time to go home, time to go home
Andy Pandy

If someone utters the words '**Time to go home**', they may well simply be telling you that it is time to leave somewhere, but if they repeat the phrase, or even start singing it, it's a fair bet that they spent a good part of their childhood watching a puppet dressed in a striped clown outfit, dating from the earliest days of children's television.

The puppet in question is Andy Pandy, who was created by Freda Lingstrom and her friend Maria Bird in 1950 in response to a request to produce a television programme along the lines of radio's *Listen with Mother*. The doll itself was made by a neighbour of Lingstrom and Bird's in the Kent village of Westerham (better known for being a former residence of Winston Churchill).

Around 40 films featuring Andy Pandy and his playmates Teddy and the rag doll Looby Loo were made between 1950 and 1959. These became a centrepiece of the BBC's regular *Watch with Mother* slot when it started up in 1953, and were repeated many times over the next two decades – so many times, in fact, that by 1970 the original films had become worn out and a new series of thirteen episodes was produced, with Andy and friends now appearing in glorious technicolour.

The films were aimed at pre-school children and consisted of a series of games and songs, with narrator Vera McKechnie inviting viewers to join in. Each episode ended with Andy and Teddy returning to their toy basket while Maria Bird sang the mournful theme song which informed the children that it was 'Time to go home' before culminating in a heartbreakingly drawn-out 'goooodbyyyye.'

Titter ye not!

Up Pompeii!

One of Frankie Howerd's favourite comic devices involved him using double and single entendres 'unintentionally' and then chastising the laughing audience for having dirty minds. This mock censoriousness is captured by one of Howerd's oft-repeated asides, '**Titter ye not!**'

Frankie Howerd was one of a number of ex-servicemen who were given the opportunity to work for the BBC after World War II by producer Dennis Main Wilson. Howerd and other comedians who had cut their comic teeth in military concert parties – Spike Milligan, Tony Hancock, Peter Sellers and Eric Sykes to name but a few – now found themselves, first on radio and then on television, amusing not just fellow soldiers but the nation at large. Despite frequent bouts of stage fright, Howerd grasped his opportunity and appeared regularly on British television screens from 1952 to his death in 1992.

He is perhaps best remembered for his performances as the Roman slave Lurcio in *Up Pompeii!* in 1969 and 1970. Scripted by *Carry On* gagman Talbot Rothwell, this bawdy show was perfectly suited to Howerd's style. Although it took the form of a sitcom, the action would frequently stop to allow Howerd to deliver monologues to the camera in the manner of a stand-up performer. Asides about the standard of the scripts and the cheapness of the sets were popular, as were various reproachful catchphrases along the lines of 'Titter ye not!' While in character, Howerd made a nod to the historical setting with the mock-Shakespearean negative phrase '**Nay, nay, and thrice nay.**'

'Titter ye not!' has become so well-known that it can often be used as the basis of puns, even by the likes of Cumbrian health officials, who recently posted a plea to the residents of Seascale to refrain from careless waste disposal under the heading 'Litter ye not!'

to boldly go
Star Trek

The most famous split infinitive in history comes from the opening voice-over to the science-fiction series *Star Trek* (see page 174). The full introduction (spoken by William Shatner in the original series) runs as follows: 'Space, the final frontier. These are the voyages of the Starship *Enterprise*. Its five-year mission: to explore strange new worlds, to seek out new life and new civilizations, **to boldly go** where no man has gone before.'

The high profile enjoyed by *Star Trek* has meant that the phrase 'to boldly go' has been seized upon and used in numerous grammar books in discussions about the acceptability of the split infinitive (the grammatical structure where an adverb – in this case 'boldly' – stands between the two words that make up the infinitive form of the verb – in this case 'to go'). For example, one book allows that it is perfectly acceptable to use a split infinitive but nevertheless cannot resist rewriting the phrase in three different ways in order to highlight that where you place the adverb can affect the meaning and rhythm: 'to boldly go where no man has gone before' has a different emphasis to 'to go boldly where no man has gone before' or 'boldly to go where no man has gone before'.

Even for writers without a grammatical axe to grind, 'to boldly go' has become a powerful phrase capable of summing up the whole idea of space exploration. NASA has picked up on it and regularly uses it in pronouncements about its future missions. However, space is not the final frontier as far as 'to boldly go' is concerned. The phrase has also been applied to pet fanciers, young scientists, football clubs, pest controllers, universities, personal computers and clergymen, to name but a few.

The catchphrase has also proved a gift to the writers of newspaper headlines. In December 2004, for example, the *Yorkshire Post* could not resist using it in a story about the return to England of Yorkshireman Patrick Stewart (who plays Captain Picard in *Star Trek: The Next Generation*) after 17 years in California. The headline: 'To boldly go where he lived before'.

Tonight, Matthew, I'm going to be ...

Stars in Their Eyes

Karaoke is big business. Starting out as a simple way for hard-working Japanese salarymen to unwind, it quickly spread worldwide and eventually became a format for a television show. The series, *Stars in Their Eyes*, has become so popular that its live final at the end of each run is one of the major non-sporting betting events of the year. For would-be stars and punters alike, the heart skips a beat whenever the words '**Tonight, Matthew, I'm going to be ...**' are heard.

Stars in Their Eyes has been a staple of Saturday-night viewing since 1990. Although first fronted by Leslie Crowther and latterly by Cat Deeley, the show is most closely associated with the long tenure of its second host, Matthew Kelly, from whom the programme's catchphrase is derived. The format is simple: five contestants compete for the votes of the studio audience by performing a rendition of a song by a famous singer. The contestants first appear in ordinary clothes for a brief chat with the host, all the time giving clues about who they will be imitating. They then introduce their act by announcing, 'Tonight, Matthew, I'm going to be Eminem/Dana/whoever', before exiting and reappearing in a cloud of dry ice, dressed and made up as their singing idol. The eventual winner gets to perform his or her song again and competes in the live final at the end of the series. Whoever wins has fifteen minutes of fame performing their act in clubland before, presumably, returning to relative obscurity.

The show's catchphrase is now widely used beyond the confines of television, either ironically to indicate that someone is a bit of an impostor in their chosen field (as when *The Guardian* suggested that underachieving Formula One star Jenson Button might appear on the show and say, 'Tonight, Matthew, I'm going to be a racing driver'), or to point out a physical resemblance to a famous person (as in the case of the football fan who persistently heckled a well-built, shaven-headed referee with the words 'Tonight, Matthew, I'm going to be Buster Bloodvessel [lead singer of 1980s band Bad Manners]' before bursting into a chorus of 'Special Brew').

Trekkie

⇨ See **Star Trek**

204

up-and-under

⇨ See **early bath**

Victor Meldrew

⇨ See **I don't believe it!**

Walkies!
Training Dogs the Woodhouse Way

In 2004, readers of the *Radio Times* voted Barbara Woodhouse number four in a poll of television's greatest eccentrics. TV's most famous dog trainer may have died in 1988, but viewers had certainly not forgotten her.

Barbara Woodhouse first appeared on British screens in 1980 with her show *Training Dogs the Woodhouse Way*, and quickly became one of the most talked about personalities on TV. Her method for training dogs was to be firm with the animal but even firmer with the owner, much to the amusement of the show's many fans. Despite being a septuagenarian, Barbara was anything but frail. She barked out her commands in a manner more suited to a Prussian parade ground than the world of pampered pooches, and woe betide any owner not copying her forceful enunciations of such commands as 'Sit!', 'Stay!' and '**Walkies!**' This last word was her characteristic way of telling a dog that it was time go for a walk, and it soon became ubiquitous.

Inevitably, this larger-than-life character has been the subject of a number of parodies. A 1991 episode of *The Simpsons* features an elderly English dog trainer called Emily Winthropp (voiced by Tracey Ullman), who bears a conspicuous resemblance to Ms Woodhouse. Then there is the comic scene from the 1983 film *Octopussy* where James Bond stumbles across a tiger while being pursued by villains in the Indian jungle. Instead of dispatching it with his trusty Walther PPK, Bond firmly commands the beast to 'Sit!', in a pointed homage to Woodhouse, before making good his escape.

walk of shame

⇨ See **You are the weakest link, goodbye**

We have the technology
The Six Million Dollar Man

The Six Million Dollar Man enjoyed a successful run on television in the 1970s with its formulaic tales of an astronaut whose shattered body has been rebuilt by science to give him superhuman 'bionic' powers (see page 17).

If some aspects of the show stretched credulity to the limits, one of its more realistic features was the opening sequence, in which the horrific accident which had occasioned this drastic surgery was re-enacted. Instead of resorting to unconvincing special effects, the show's makers ran footage from a real crash in 1967 involving test pilot Bruce Petersen. The opening sequence also featured a voice-over which summed up the premise of the show: 'Steve Austin, astronaut. A man barely alive. Gentlemen, we can rebuild him. We have the technology. We have the capability to build the world's first bionic man. Steve Austin will be that man. Better than he was before. Better, stronger, faster.'

Repeated every week, the introduction quickly got under the skin of the show's viewers. Indeed the phrase '**We have the technology**' has outlived Steve Austin by many years, being used jocularly as a response to such questions as 'Are you able to fix the lawnmower?' and 'Can you get the car started?' The longevity of the phrase was illustrated when, some twenty-five years after the final episode of *The Six Million Dollar Man*, 'We have the technology … we can rebuild' was used by *The Scotsman* in the headline of a report about the rebuilding of Edinburgh's Old Town following a fire.

We'll have no trouble here!

⇨ See **a local shop for local people**

We're doomed!

⇨ See **Dad's Army**

whack
The Sopranos

The mob drama *The Sopranos* (see page 190) abounds in American criminal slang, but one word has struck a particular chord with its viewers and become emblematic of the show. Although Tony Soprano and his associates have any number of ways of referring to the act of murder ('clip', 'hit', 'pop' and 'burn' for starters), their term of choice is '**whack**'. This word is so expressive that fans of the show can often be heard repeating it with relish and conversing in online chatrooms about which character will be the next to get 'whacked'. Such has been the popularity of the expression that by the time *The Sopranos* began its fifth series, an Indianapolis newspaper could herald the show's return with the headline 'Whack is back'.

The term has caught on in Britain no less than in the United States. Indeed, it would not now be surprising to hear characters in *The Bill* or *Taggart* talking of a villain being 'whacked', although the term has yet to be heard in the more genteel environment of *The Midsomer Murders*.

What do you think of it so far? – Rubbish!

The Morecambe and Wise Show

The double-act of Eric Morecambe and Ernie Wise lasted over four decades from 1941, when they worked together in music hall, until Morecambe's death in 1984. Working with scriptwriter Eddie Braben, they became one of the UK's all-time favourite comedy acts.

They recorded 100 episodes of *The Morecambe and Wise Show* for ITV (1961–68 and 1978–83), in between which were 69 shows for the BBC (1968–77) in what is generally regarded as their golden period. The shows combined sketches with elements of stand-up and situation comedy, with the duo appearing together in front of a safety curtain at various points in the show to link the whole thing together. In general, Wise was the naive and egotistical straight man while Morecambe was the childlike and cocky funny man, and they played off each other effortlessly.

A central conceit in their act was Wise's aspiration to be a great playwright. This allowed the cast to play out parodies of TV costume drama with bad dialogue and cheap props, often using a celebrity guest. These guests included Peter Cushing, Glenda Jackson, André Previn, Diana Rigg, Shirley Bassey and Eric Porter, with a common joke being that the duo pretended not to have heard of them, or confused them with someone else. Eric, ever the show-off, would clown around and try to steal the show, most commonly by pausing briefly during the proceedings to ask a prop such as a statue or a stuffed toy, '**What do you think of it so far?**', to which the answer from the prop, animated by Eric, would be, '**Rubbish!**' – a gag he first worked in a spoof of *Antony and Cleopatra*, using a portrait bust as a ventriloquist's dummy to upstage guest star Glenda Jackson.

This call-and-response routine went down so well that it was repeated in subsequent shows, and the words are still used to pass judgement on any activity that has started badly and shows little promise of improvement.

⇨ See also **short fat hairy legs**

Where's me washboard?

The Fast Show

Stand-up comedy is not what it used to be. For that we can only be grateful if **'Where's me washboard?'** is indicative of the quality of humour that flourished among the music-hall turns of the 1940s.

This parody of a catchphrase belonged to the fictional Arthur Atkinson, cheeky Cockney singer, dancer, comic and all-round favourite of music hall, created by Paul Whitehouse for *The Fast Show* (see page 183). The character appeared in what purported to be old black-and-white archive footage, looking dapper in a striped suit and felt hat. Arthur's arrival on stage would be greeted by rapturous applause from his adoring audience, and his every utterance, no matter how nonsensical or vaguely but personally insulting towards audience members, would give rise to uproarious laughter. His trademark phrase 'Where's me washboard?' was always received with particular delight.

Modern television viewers have rather different expectations of their comedians, and they are often bemused by the fact that comics of the past should have been able to raise a laugh simply by saying 'Can I do you now, sir?' or 'I don't mind if I do.' For this generation, 'Where's me washboard?' has come to sum up an absurdly overrated and mercifully defunct strand of the comic tradition.

... which was nice
The Fast Show

The British are renowned for having both an aptitude for understatement and a passion for pleasantness. Therefore to make an outlandish claim about a famous rock band playing an impromptu concert in one's garden only to tack on the phrase '**... which was nice**' may seem to some to be merely an extreme example of a typically British sort of attitude.

Fortunately, the British also have a reputation for laughing at their own foibles. So when Patrick Nice, a character played by Mark Williams in *The Fast Show* (see page 183), who embodies 'niceness' to such an extent that he has been named after it, tagged every ludicrous claim he made from his comfortable kitchen in suburban Middle England with '... which was nice', the public got the joke, and started using the phrase in the same way – which was nice.

" ... and I was rummaging around in the attic, and I found the original copy of the Bible — which was nice."

Who do you think you are kidding, Mr Hitler?
⇨ See **Dad's Army**

Who lives in a house like this?

Through the Keyhole

If you want to register your surprise at how palatial, or more usually how shabby, a particular house is, you might ask, '**Who lives in a house like this?**' The phrase will be forever associated with Loyd Grossman, celebrity purveyor of fine bottled sauces and erstwhile house detective on the BBC panel game *Through the Keyhole*.

In this light-hearted show, presented by Sir David Frost, panellists attempt to identify a mystery celebrity from a video tour of his or her house. The chairman gets the proceedings going, and gives the studio audience and the viewers a glimpse of the house's owner, then hands over to a sidekick who conducts a tour of the house, drawing attention to objects that may hint at the owner's identity or may be complete red herrings.

Since 2002, the sidekick has been Catherine Gee, but the role was originally and memorably played by Boston-born Loyd Grossman, whose curiously drawling delivery and ostentatiously paraded knowledge of art and architecture made him an impressionist's gift. At the end of each tour, Grossman would summarize the 'evidence', then hand back to the studio with the never-changing formula, 'Who lives in a house like this? David, it's over to you.'

The expression is eminently flexible and can be adapted to show admiration, or more usually disgust, for the owner of almost anything, as in 'Who sits at a desk like this?' or 'Who's been sleeping in a bed like this?' It can also be given a more personal edge: 'Who would go out with a guy like this?'

Who loves ya, baby?

⇨ See **Kojak**

whoopsie

⇨ See **Ooh, Betty**

Who Wants to Be a Millionaire?

Most British quiz shows are fairly sedate affairs. Little except personal pride is at stake and prizes are usually modest. *Who Wants to Be a Millionaire?* is a very different kind of quiz show. Life-changing sums are on offer and even an appearance at the High Court is not out of the question.

Debuting in Britain in 1998, the show quickly attained massive public interest. Based on the simple idea that prize money is doubled (more or less) every time a question is answered correctly, Chris Tarrant's quiz has proved compulsive viewing. Fifteen multiple-choice general-knowledge questions must be tackled to win a cool million, with the questions getting more difficult as the potential prize money increases.

Contestants are helped in their quest by being given three 'lifelines': a '50:50' results in two of the four possible answers being removed from the screen in order to reduce the odds of a successful answer to evens; 'ask the audience' permits the contestant to look at the results of electronic voting by the studio audience; '**phone a friend**' allows the contestant to phone a colleague, friend, or family member who will, it is hoped, provide him or her with the correct answer. This final lifeline has become something of a catchphrase in Britain, and anyone put on the spot by a difficult question at, say, a job interview can defuse the tension by saying 'Can I phone a friend?'

Another catchphrase popularized by the show is '**But we don't want to give you that**.' These are the words habitually used by host Chris Tarrant when showing contestants the cheque they have just won, while reminding them that everyone would prefer to see a much larger sum pocketed.

While many quiz shows are based around the speed with which a question is answered, the hot-seat stage of *Who Wants to Be a Millionaire?* hooks viewers by prolonging the time a contestant spends mulling the answer. Those in the hot seat are encouraged to take their time and think things through. They often change their minds and go through agonies before offering an answer. At this stage Tarrant is apt to ask them, '**Is that your final answer?**' This question often creates further indecision and still more tension before the contestant finally provides their definitive answer.

The impact made by the show and its catchphrases on the public imagination can perhaps be summed up by the following joke: a husband and wife are watching *Who Wants to Be a Millionaire*, and the husband winks and says, 'Honey, let's go upstairs ...' The wife says no. A minute later the husband asks again. Again she says no. So the husband says, 'Is that your final answer?' The wife says yes. The husband says, 'Well, can I phone a friend?'

One particular edition of *Millionaire* was no laughing matter. In September 2001, Major Charles Ingram won the jackpot prize of £1 million. Later, however, it was revealed that his success was not entirely the product of his own brilliance. Ingram had answered the questions using help from two people in the audience who had used loud coughs to indicate the correct answers. The three – Ingram, his wife Diana and their improbably named co-conspirator Tecwen Whittock – were found guilty of procuring the execution of a valuable security by deception, fined heavily and given suspended prison sentences. Plans are afoot to make a film of the remarkable events, although the convicted trio still protest their innocence.

Who was that masked man?

The Lone Ranger

If someone makes a brief appearance before disappearing with indecent haste, it might well prompt the jocular question '**Who was that masked man?**' The phrase is, of course, an allusion to the Western series *The Lone Ranger*. At the end of each episode one of the bystanders would inevitably turn to another and ask, 'Who was that masked man?' The equally formulaic reply was always, 'Why, that was the Lone Ranger!'

The Lone Ranger was a popular radio serial before it made the transition to television in 1956, ending its run in 1962. The hero, played on TV by Clayton Moore, was a kind of cowboy Robin Hood, roaming the West righting wrongs and defending the weak against the villainous, always hiding his identity behind a black eye-mask. He was accompanied on his adventures by two constant companions, one being the devoted Native American scout Tonto (played by Jay Silverheels), and the other being his beautiful white horse Silver, whom the Lone Ranger would spur into action using the show's other catchphrase: 'Hi-yo Silver, away!'

No dirty realism was involved in this show: the hero was always immaculate, down to his trademark white hat and silver bullets, and he never shot to kill, being a master of shooting the guns out of the bad guys' hands. The theme music for the show was based on the overture to Rossini's *William Tell* and it was a popular wisecrack that you could define an intellectual as a person who heard that music and thought of the opera rather than *The Lone Ranger*.

With my reputation?

The Fast Show

The rakish 13th Duke of Wybourne, played by Paul Whitehouse, was one of the most popular characters to appear on *The Fast Show* (see page 183). Dressed in his smoking jacket, a bottle of champagne in his hand, this blue-blooded Lothario was often caught by the camera in locations that offered ample opportunity for sexual conquest. With crisp upper-class intonation and a knowing leer, the Duke would inform viewers of his whereabouts, adding in astonishment at his good fortune, '**With my reputation?**'

In imitation of this, anyone who is exposed to great temptation might comment on the event with the ironic rhetorical question, 'Me? With my reputation?' Or the phrase may be delivered with mock indignation, as a riposte to any suggestion that is at odds with one's personality ('Me? Watch a costume drama? With my reputation?').

"Me, the 13th Duke of Wybourne? Here? In a student nurses' hall of residence? With my reputation?"

We are clearly meant to believe that Paul Whitehouse's dashing duke is a notorious womanizer with a reputation that is far less honourable than his title. In the real world, however, the catchphrase is often employed by those whose less colourful reputations are unlikely to precede them.

Wudayagonnado?

⇨ See **The Sopranos**

Yabba-dabba-doo!

The Flintstones

The American cartoon show *The Flintstones* first aired in September 1960 on ABC and ran for six seasons and 166 episodes. The final episode aired in April 1966, with reruns lasting until September. NBC re-broadcast the series from January 1967 through to August 1969, and again from September 1969 to September 1970. To this day, fans can still see the show practically every day on many channels around the world.

Makers William Hanna and Joseph Barbera and their team experimented with different sorts of cartoon family before hitting on the idea of cavemen and their 'modern stone-age' appliances. The original working title was 'the Flagstones', but this was eventually changed, and what emerged was a two-family relationship between Fred and Wilma Flintstone with their daughter Pebbles, and Barney and Betty Rubble and their son Bamm-Bamm.

The phrase '**Yabba-dabba-doo!**' was frequently used by Fred Flintstone as an expression of delight, triumph or excitement and has carried over into modern culture, being used over the years by successive generations of fans. It came from Alan Reed, the voice of Fred (the voice of Barney being the great Mel Blanc – see page 181). According to Joe Barbera, during one of the recording sessions Reed asked, 'Where it says "Yahoo", can I say "Yabba-dabba-doo"?' Barbera assented, and that was that. Reed said that the idea for the phrase came from his mother, who used to say, 'A little dab'll do ya', a line she seems to have borrowed from a Brylcreem commercial.

> When you're with the Flintstones
> Have a yabba-dabba-doo time,
> A dabba-doo time.
> You'll have a gay old time.

yada yada yada

Seinfeld

The US sitcom *Seinfeld* was famously supposed to be about nothing. Well, it was really about Jerry Seinfeld and his friends and … **yada yada yada**. This phrase, meaning essentially 'and so on' or 'blah blah blah' was not new (*The Chambers Dictionary* suggests it may derive from the Hebrew *yada*, meaning 'knowledge'), but it was certainly brought to a wider audience by this show, which was broadcast between 1990 and 1998.

The format for the show was usually the same: Seinfeld performed parts of his stand-up comedy routine over the opening credits before the show's cast began to act out the drama in Jerry's apartment, a restaurant or some other Manhattan location. Nothing much would happen in the way of action; this show was all about the comic dialogue and complex interplay between the cast of friends. These were the wry and neurotic Jerry Seinfeld (played by himself), the wacky and relationship-troubled Elaine (Julia Louis-Dreyfus), the sex-obsessed dreamer George (Jason Alexander) and Seinfeld's eccentric neighbour Kramer (Michael Richards).

> "Well, we were engaged to be married, uh, we bought the wedding invitations, and, uh, yada yada yada, I'm still single."

The 'yada yada yada' phrase was really a kind of verbal shorthand, allowing the characters to skip the dull (or embarrassing) parts of their conversation and 'cut to the chase'. It formed the title of an episode ('The Yada Yada', broadcast in April 1997) in which among other lines George, in reply to being asked if he was close to his parents, said, 'Well, they gave birth to me and … yada yada yada.'

You are awful

The Dick Emery Show

The Dick Emery Show holds the record as the BBC's longest-running sketch show, and for many years it started off with a series of spoof vox-pop interviews in which all the interviewees were comic characters played by Emery himself. One such was a busty blonde called Mandy, who would always be asked questions involving outrageous double-entendres by the straight-man interviewer. After each question she would widen her eyes in surprise and say, 'I beg your pardon?', and the flustered interviewer would then rephrase his question in a way which turned out to be even ruder. Eventually Mandy would pout, smile, and say in a low voice, 'Ooh, you are awful – but I like you' before giving the interviewer a friendly shove that would send him flying. The catchphrase '**You are awful**' became popular as an expression of reluctant approval, often used to convey one's amusement at a cruel remark that the speaker knows they ought to censure, but which he or she cannot help finding funny. It was also used in the title of Emery's 1972 film based on his TV characters.

Dick Emery was born into a theatrical family in London in 1917. After early work in the theatre, he began getting regular work on BBC radio and started to develop a repertoire of characters, some of whom would re-emerge later in his TV show. He made the switch to television in 1963 and *The Dick Emery Show* ran on the BBC until 1979, when it switched to ITV for a further two years as *The Dick Emery Comedy Hour*. Besides Mandy, the show featured many characters who became national favourites, including a sexually frustrated spinster called Hettie who would always ask the interviewer, 'Are you married?', a vicar with outrageously prominent teeth, and an upper-class tramp called College.

The idea of a sketch show featuring a series of regular characters all played by a single actor has proved influential, and Emery is often cited as an influence on later character-based sketch shows such as *Harry Enfield's Television Programme* (see page 62), *The Fast Show* (see page 183) and *Goodness Gracious Me* (see page 31).

You are the weakest link, goodbye

The Weakest Link

Most game shows employ a genial host to encourage contestants, applaud their triumphs and sympathize with their shortcomings. This formula was neatly turned on its head in 2000 when the BBC introduced *The Weakest Link*, with its acerbic host, Anne Robinson, whose role was to be as nasty as possible to contestants, dismissing losers with the brusque catchphrase, '**You are the weakest link, goodbye**.'

The show worked by getting a 'team' of contestants to answer questions to contribute to a common pool of prize money. At the end of each round, one contestant was eliminated, with all team members being asked to vote on the individual they thought had performed least well. This, of course, allowed a certain amount of tactical voting, with contestants trying to get rid of rivals rather than honestly promoting the survival of the fittest. As host, Anne Robinson would positively encourage the players to turn on one another, with such remarks as 'One of you is not pulling your weight' or 'Who is consistently letting you down?' This was just part of a routine which also involved belittling participants with barbs such as 'Do you not get out much?', before finally telling them, 'You leave with nothing.'

Dismissed contestants would be shown getting down from the podium and walking off set past the camera, a humiliating process that became known as the '**walk of shame**'.

Before the year was out, the catchphrase 'You are the weakest link' had caught the public's imagination and could be heard in playgrounds and pubs around the country. It was even used by Prime Minister Tony Blair to mock opposition leader William Hague during House-of-Commons debate. Blair himself had been dubbed 'the weakest link' shortly before that by protesters angry about the price of petrol.

Anne Robinson also fronted the American version of show, and her abrasive attitude was even more shocking to mollycoddled American contestants. The format has also been extended to various special editions, such as those with all-celebrity panels of players and one show in the United States where all of the players were Elvis impersonators.

You dirty old man!

Steptoe and Son

There can be few comic characters with more repugnant personal habits than Albert Steptoe. The senior partner of Britain's favourite pair of rag-and-bone-men would think nothing of retrieving pickled onions from his bathwater and putting them back in the jar, much to his son Harold's disgust. Harold, always trying to rise above his humble origins, would bemoan his father's unhygienic acts and frequent lewd comments, giving rise to *Steptoe and Son*'s only catchphrase, '**You dirty old man!**'

First broadcast in 1962, and finishing with a Christmas special in 1974, *Steptoe and Son* is one the BBC's best loved and most critically acclaimed sitcoms. Writers Ray Galton and Alan Simpson, who had recently had their services dispensed with by Tony Hancock, penned what they thought would be a one-off show about two rag-and-bone-men. It was a hit and the Corporation commissioned a series with Wilfrid Brambell as Albert and Harry H Corbett as Harold. The show straddled the black-and-white and colour eras, garnering critical plaudits as well as huge ratings. *Steptoe and Son* had a dark side and was laced with pathos: Harold's plans to improve himself and to mix with a better class of people are invariably ruined by the intervention of his dad, but Harold's resentment of his father is always outweighed by familial bonds which keep him trapped in Albert's ramshackle house in Oil Drum Lane, Shepherd's Bush.

Harold's famous rebuke has often been borrowed in later times. Probably the most notorious instance of this was in Bill Grundy's 1976 television interview with The Sex Pistols. The veteran broadcaster was not getting much of a response from the punk rockers and so turned his attentions to the band's groupie – and future star in her own right – Siouxsie Sioux. Feeling that she had warmed to him, Grundy suggested jokingly that he meet her after the show. Shocked by the impropriety of the offer, guitarist Steve Jones exclaimed, 'You dirty sod! You dirty old man!' and, egged on by Grundy, famously continued his insults with industrial language not appropriate for tea-time television or this book.

You don't want to do that!

⇨ See **Harry Enfield's Television Programme**

You get nothing for a pair ... not in this game

⇨ See **Points make prizes**

You might say that; I couldn't possibly comment

House of Cards

The world of ruthless political ambition was memorably personified by Francis Urquhart. A government Chief Whip who eventually became Prime Minister, Urquhart's Machiavellian methods would have made the Borgias blush. Behind the scenes he was brutal, but in public he was charmingly enigmatic, using ambiguous answers in reply to any question that put him on the spot. His typical delphic response to an assertion by a journalist, opponent or, indeed, a colleague was '**You might say that; I couldn't possibly comment**.'

House of Cards was a novel by Michael Dobbs that was adapted for BBC television in 1990 by Andrew Davies. Ian Richardson played Francis Urquhart, the man whose initials summed up his political philosophy. The adaptation was notable for its use of the dramatic device of letting the protagonist address the audience with asides. This meant that viewers felt somehow complicit in Urquhart's misdeeds, which even went as far as murdering investigative journalist Mattie Storin (Susannah Harker).

Urquhart's phrase quickly became part of the lexicon of British politics although, because of its origins, it is only used by speakers in a knowing or mischievous way. In 2001, after a series of scandals that rocked the fledgling Holyrood parliament, the BBC's political correspondent north of the border remarked, 'The political scene in Scotland is fast becoming like an episode from *House of Cards* ... Is it all oscillating between tragedy, crisis and farce? You might say that. I couldn't possibly comment.'

Your boys took a hell of a beating

NRK Sport

It is September 1981 and veteran broadcaster Bjørge Lillelien is commentating for the Norwegian channel NRK on a World Cup qualifying match in Oslo between Norway and England. England has won all five previous football matches between the two countries by wide margins, so it is a huge surprise when the home team pulls off a 2–1 victory. Most commentators could be relied upon on to greet such an occasion by launching into a stirring patriotic broadside, but Lillelien surpasses all expectations. Switching from Norwegian into English, he takes the opportunity to harangue some of the vanquished country's most famous historical and contemporary figures: 'Lord Nelson! Lord Beaverbrook! Sir Winston Churchill! Sir Anthony Eden! Clement Attlee! Henry Cooper! Lady Diana! Maggie Thatcher! Can you hear me? Maggie Thatcher! Your boys took a hell of a beating! Your boys took a hell of a beating!'

In the aftermath of the game, Lillelien's demented commentary was repeated on British television, and the phrase '**Your boys took a hell of a beating**', preceded by a roll-call of names, came to be regarded as a classic way of rubbing the losers' noses in it. The commentary was even parodied in the finale of the 2001 film *The Mean Machine*.

His bizarre outburst secured a measure of broadcasting immortality for Bjørge Lillelien. Twenty years later, *The Guardian* listed it as number one in its top ten sporting commentaries of all time. However, the 1981 game was to prove the high-water mark of a career that later descended into self-parody. By the time of his death in 1987, he was regarded in Norway as more of a national joke than a national treasure.

Index of television programmes

Note that all programmes whose titles begin with 'The' can be found under T in this index.

Also from Chambers...

The Chambers Dictionary

The Chambers Dictionary remains the dictionary of choice for professional writers, puzzle and wordgame enthusiasts and everyone with a love of words. This thoroughly revised edition contains over 10,000 new words and meanings, including nearly 3,000 new main entry words. While the traditional Chambers virtues of being informative, witty and authoritative have been retained, the design and content have been updated to provide a clear and modern text for today's users.

- More words and definitions than any other single-volume English dictionary
- Thoroughly revised and updated to reflect modern usage
- The richest range of English from Shakespeare to the present day
- Clear, accurate and, on occasion, characteristically witty definitions
- Unequalled inclusion of literary and obscure words from the past
- Extensive appendices including first names, foreign phrases and scientific information
- Preface by Melvyn Bragg

Standard ♦ **£30.00** ♦ 0550 10013 X

Thumb-Indexed ♦ **£35.00** ♦ 0550 10105 5

Hardback ♦ 1856pp ♦ 268 x 178mm

Vitamin Q
by Roddy Lumsden

a temple of trivia lists
and curious words

Roddy Lumsden

This diverse collection mixes quirky lists, intriguing facts and
playful reflections into a unique and informative brew that's
entertaining, thought-provoking and utterly absorbing. A temple
of trivia lists and curious words, *Vitamin Q* is based, in part,
upon the cult website of the same name, but the lists have been
revised and expanded to include even more curiosities from
around the world.

- Why did our ancestors leap over dead donkeys?
- When should you eat rabbit droppings?
- Which 13 things do we inevitably discuss in bars?
- Who wrote 'Ode on the Mammoth Cheese'?
- What kind of creature is the *bloody trivia*?

£9.99 ◆ 0550 10145 4 ◆ Paperback ◆ 368pp ◆ 216 x 128mm